TRUE FRIENDSHIP

JOHN CUDDEBACK

True Friendship

Where Virtue Becomes Happiness

IGNATIUS PRESS   SAN FRANCISCO

Cover photograph by Austin Kehmeier/Unsplash

Cover design by Enrique J. Aguilar

© 2021 by Ignatius Press, San Francisco
All rights reserved
ISBN 978-1-62164-355-5 (PB)
ISBN 978-1-64229-149-0 (eBook)
Library of Congress Control Number 2020946173
Printed in the United States of America ∞

Contents

Foreword by Curtis Martin 7

Preface to the Second Edition 11

1. Happiness and Friendship 13
2. Friendship and Its Kinds 33
3. Friendship and Self-Image 51
4. Friendship and Virtue: Moral and
   Intellectual 63
5. Friendship and Society 75
6. Discerning and Testing Friendship:
   The Wisdom of Saint Aelred 85
7. Dating, Marriage, and Friendship 99
8. Friendship with Parents, Teachers, and
   Mentors 113
9. Charity: Friendship with God and
   Neighbor 123

Epilogue: Friendship in This Life and in
   the Next 137

A Gospel Meditation 141

Sources Cited 145

Further Reading 147

Foreword

Searching history, both secular and sacred, one is hard-pressed to find examples of authentic friendship. There are certainly great people and great achievements, but what about great friendships? Yes, we see the loyalty of Jonathan, who, despite the fact that he is the heir apparent to the throne of Israel, prefers faithfulness to David over personal power (1 Sam 18–20). It is inspiring to see Elisha's fidelity to Elijah—unwilling to leave his mentor's side until the latter is carried away to heaven in a chariot of fire (2 Kings 2). But in history, betrayal seems more typical than genuine friendship: Jesus is betrayed by one of his apostles, Brutus betrays his Caesar, and even in legend, Lancelot betrays King Arthur.

We should not be astonished that something so important to each of us is also so difficult to achieve. Original Sin did not merely force the human family to relocate; it sent a devastating rift into our relationships—with God and with one another. Only moments after the Fall, man and woman were at odds with each other, and within a generation, their children were killing one another. Ever since, it seems, this world has offered more heartache than consolation when it comes to relationships.

So where can we turn to find authentic friendship? Ancients, such as Plato and Aristotle, tell us about friendship. Jesus gives us the power to live it. The proof is right there in history. If we peel back our sometimes overly pious perceptions of the saints, we will see something amazing—they almost always come in clusters. It is not by accident that when we think of Saint Augustine, we think of Monica and Ambrose; when we think of Saint Francis, we think of Clare and Brother Bernard; and when we think of Saint Ignatius of Loyola, we think of Francis Xavier. These Christians lived in the power of Christ and realized the joy of the restored ability to live in friendship with God and with one another. This ability can be yours as well, if you learn how to forge friendship.

Of all that we desire in life, friendship has a unique place. Indeed, can there even be happiness without friendship? What if you had all that the world could offer—such as health, wealth, and reputation—but no one to share it with? Every evening you were graced with a perfect sunset, but you could never say to a friend, "Look, isn't it beautiful?" Friendship is the crowning gift of happiness. But it does not stop there. Friendship proves itself in suffering: "A friend loves at all times, and a brother is born for adversity" (Prov 17:17). Even when wealth disappears, or health departs, a friend can soften the pain. And what can compare to the sting of being betrayed by a close friend? Friendship is not merely part of a good life—it is at the heart of what it means to live life to the full.

Our hearts tell us that we are made for friendship, and there is a reality that corresponds to our desire, but how do we realize it? John Cuddeback has given us a great tool: *True Friendship*. Authentic friendship does not just happen—it is an art that must be learned, a skill that must be practiced. *True Friendship* shows us the wisdom of the ancients, what the most admirable women and men of the past have learned about forging friendships that will endure.

But there is more. We need more than a roadmap; we need

assistance in following the path. At times, something within us hinders us from doing even what we know is right. If we look honestly at ourselves, we find a gap between what we are and what we know we ought to be. Bridging this gap is a necessary precondition to finding genuine friendship. This is precisely the genius of this book; providing more than answers, it points us toward the antidote.

We find ourselves hungering for friendship not only with a brother or a sister, but, in a deeper place, with God. "You have made us for yourself, and our hearts are restless until they rest in you", says Saint Augustine in his *Confessions*. The actions of Christ anticipate the hunger in our hearts. Jesus comes to us with an offer of friendship: "No longer do I call you servants . . . but I have called you friends" (Jn 15:15). His gracious initiative starts us on the path to friendship; he is the creative artist of our hearts, and with his presence in our lives, we begin to live the art of friendship. Where we are blind, he brings light; where we are broken, he brings healing; and where we are alone, he comes to us. "I have loved you with an everlasting love" (Jer 31:3).

It is within the friendship of Christ that we may begin to form friendships with others. Saint Paul rejoices in this radical freedom to live friendship when he reminds the Christians at Thessalonica, "Being affectionately desirous of you, we were ready to share with you not only the gospel of God but also our own selves, because you had become very dear to us." (1 Thess 2:8). This is the freedom we have in Christ —to live life to the full. Yes, in this world we will find trials and tribulations, but we need not be alone. Friendship magnifies our joy and can bear us through life's difficulties. Can there be anything more important than learning how to become a true friend?

— Curtis Martin

Preface to the Second Edition

Early in the new millennium, a relatively new campus ministry organization (FOCUS) asked me to write a book on friendship. The first few years of their work with young people in college had made clear a serious problem: a lack of understanding of friendship—its nature, its kinds, its importance. Many young people knew they were missing something, but they did not know what, or how to get it. They felt disconnected and lost.

I had already been teaching Aristotle and Saint Thomas Aquinas on friendship to my college students for a few years, and I had seen in that short time that the truth about friendship changes lives. So I wrote the first edition of this book.

If life has taught me something in the intervening decade and a half, it might be this: to know something about true friendship is one thing, and to live it is another. Life tends to humble us. At the same time, it teaches us that the truths of reality are even better than we realize, if we have eyes to see it. My conviction that the truth about friendship is simply life changing has only gotten deeper.

In the intervening years, I have also begun to appreciate a lesser-known aspect of Aristotle's and Saint Thomas' thoughts on friendship—namely, how there can be friendship between parents and children and between teachers and students. This too has changed my life, even as the concrete circumstances of my life have changed. I am very happy to add a chapter on this important topic.

The other new chapter is on Saint Aelred. Here I explore his understanding of human friendship as central to God's plan for our lives—an astoundingly beautiful notion. I also try to unpack his very concrete, practical plan for what to look for in discerning friendship.

The new millennium is a time for hope and renewal, even as the prevailing culture has continued to undermine systematically the understanding, practices, and contexts of true friendship. This is a serious threat to all of us, young and old. In the last fifteen years, the changes in communication technology in particular have had dramatic effects on all of us, but especially on a generation whose habits have been formed with a hand-held device at its side. We have not really begun to reckon with the consequences.

Though this book was originally geared toward the young and will still speak powerfully to them, this revised edition is for all ages. The truth about friendship will give us a compass to navigate troubled waters. It will give us principles for understanding and responding to the pressing challenges of relationships at home, at work, and all around us.

Studying these realities has been a signal blessing in my life. Sharing them here is a privilege.

I invite you to visit my blog at Life-Craft.org.

I

Happiness and Friendship

There is nothing so precious as a faithful friend, and no scales can measure his excellence.

— Sirach 6:15

Susan could hardly believe what had just happened. She had known Mary since second grade. After all they had been through, how could it come to this? The words kept ringing in her ears: "You're just going to have to lie to your father. That's all there is to it."

On the way home from a party, Susan had crossed the median and wrecked her car, or rather, her father's car. She had promised him that she would never drink and drive, and she had always kept her word. Until now. That night, she and Mary had been drinking. Surely her father would want to know. What was she to do? She had never lied to her father, and though she was tempted, she did not want to start now. She knew that lying would be wrong.

But Mary insisted. If Susan told her father the truth, then Mary's father would find out too. The consequences would be serious, so Mary would not budge. "I don't want to have to say this, but if you tell your father, our friendship is over." All at once, Susan wondered whether she and Mary really had a friendship at all.

Most of us assume that we know what friends are. Friends are people we want to be with; they are those whom we care for and who care for us. Indeed, at times we speak with great confidence about "true friendship" and how wonderful it is. Very few people think that they do not have friends. Even fewer think that they are not able to have friends.

Many conclude that all persons, regardless of how they live, can have true friendship. Others conclude that only the most evil people are incapable of true friendship. These conclusions are mistaken. They are myths. And anyone who wants true friendship should come to see why. The reality is that true friendship is for those who live a certain kind of life.

Anyone can live this kind of life. If we want to have true friendship—indeed, if we want to be happy—we must strive to live this kind of life.

It should not be a great surprise that many of us think we have true friendships, while in reality we do not. Scripture points out that many live in a state of self-deception. In his first letter, the apostle John speaks very directly: "If we say we have fellowship with him while we walk in darkness, we lie and do not live according to the truth." He continues: "He who says 'I know him' but disobeys his commandments is a liar" (1 Jn 1:6; 2:4). Clearly, there are many of us who think that we "have fellowship" with Jesus Christ, or that we "know him", while in reality we do not. Similarly, there are many of us who think we have true friendships, while in reality we do not.

Of course, the critical question is: Why do we not have true friendships? The answer is startlingly simple. We cannot have true friendships *if we are not striving to be virtuous.* The kind of life required for friendship is a virtuous life.

Not very many people in our society would claim that they know what virtue is or that they practice it. The lack of virtue does not seem to bother them. But friendship is another matter. Friendship, more so than virtue, is valued in our society. As mentioned, most people think that they know what friendship is, and that they have it. Susan and Mary have been quite sure that they are the best of friends. But to attempt to have friendship in the absence of virtue is self-defeating. To see this point is to see one of the most profound problems of contemporary society.

The main point of this book is to examine a bedrock truth of pre-Christian *and* Christian civilization: true friendship and virtue are *inseparable*; you cannot have one without the other. Together, they are the key to human happiness.

The Wisdom of the Ancients on Virtue and Happiness

To begin our inquiry into friendship, it will be helpful to lay some groundwork with a brief examination of virtue and happiness. To do this, we will turn to a source to which the greatest Christian thinkers have often turned—the ancient Greeks.

In teaching philosophy at the college level, I find great joy in introducing students to the wisdom of the ancients, particularly their understanding of what constitutes a well-lived, or happy, life. In one of the best passages of philosophical literature, Socrates makes a defense of his way of life before the Athenian judges who are about to condemn him to death. He anticipates an offer from the jury to let him go free on the condition that he no longer practice philosophy. Socrates proceeds to explain:

> Gentlemen of the jury, I am grateful and I am your friend, but I will obey the god rather than you, and as long as I draw breath and am able, I shall not cease to practice philosophy, to exhort you and in my usual way to point out

to any one of you whom I happen to meet: "Good Sir, you are an Athenian, a citizen of the greatest city with the greatest reputation for both wisdom and power; are you not ashamed of your eagerness to possess as much wealth, reputation and honor as possible, while you do not care for nor give thought to wisdom or truth, or the best possible state of your soul?" Then, if one of you disputes this and says he does care, I shall not let him go at once or leave him, but I shall question him, examine him and test him, and if I do not think he has attained the goodness that he says he has, I shall reproach him because he attaches little importance to the most important things and greater importance to inferior things.[1]

I take this last thought as representative of a pivotal insight in Socrates' thought, an insight shared by Plato and Aristotle. The key questions about a person's way of life are these: Does the person understand what is truly most important, and does the person live in a way that reflects this understanding? To live as though what is most important is really most important is to live an ordered and happy life. To live as though inferior things are most important is to live a disordered, unhappy life. The great Greek philosophers had a profound appreciation for the nobility of a human life well lived and the tragedy of a life not well lived.

But what, in fact, are the higher, or most important, things in life? In his response to the jury, Socrates indicates that these things include wisdom, truth, and "the best possible state of your soul". According to Socrates, man has a soul, which is higher and nobler than the body. This insight is critical. If the body is what is highest in a person, then what is the point of life—to be physically fit, or to be healthy and wealthy? Something deep inside the person cries out

[1] *Apology* 29d–30a.

that there is much more. This leads to the further insight that simply flourishing bodily cannot constitute living well for a person (although it does for a bird or a horse), since there are higher human goods—those of the soul. This is where the notion of "virtue" comes in.

The Greek word for virtue, ἀρετή (*areté*), means "excellence". The philosophers insist that virtues, which are excellences of the soul, are the highest human goods. Virtues such as justice, courage, and wisdom are habits—dispositions deep in the soul—of living out what it means to be human. Therefore, to live a good, or happy, life is to live a life of virtue. All people live, but only some—those who live the life of virtue—live well. Thus, in Socrates' immortal words: "The most important thing is not life, but the good life."[2] In other words, human life is not just about being alive in body; it is about *living well*. And living well for man means first and foremost to have excellence in the soul, or to live virtuously.

Socrates was absorbed with the dismaying fact that so few people actually live good lives. There is a paradox here. On the one hand, there are few who explicitly believe that true human happiness consists in the fulfillment of bodily desires. Most people will grant that there are "goods of the soul" that are more important. Indeed, who would want to be praised at one's funeral for being fit or wealthy? Surely, we want to be remembered for some higher qualities. And who has not experienced the deep emptiness at the end of a day lived as though bodily pleasures were what brings happiness? On the other hand, how many people truly live as though what is most important is really most important? It seems that Socrates' reproach to the Athenians applies to

[2] *Crito* 48b.

many of us who say that we *know* what is most important: "Are you not ashamed of your eagerness to possess as much wealth, reputation and honor as possible, while you do not care for nor give thought to wisdom or truth, or the *best* possible state of your soul?" Socrates was very concerned about this matter. We should be too. As he says later in his trial: "It is not difficult to avoid death, gentlemen of the jury; it is much more difficult to avoid wickedness, for it runs faster than death."[3]

Living a virtuous life requires much more than just *knowing* what is most important. Virtues are all about *living out* the truth that you know. Aristotle, who was a student of Plato, who was in turn a student of Socrates, is the philosopher who gives us the most developed understanding of the virtuous life. In his masterpiece of morals, the *Nicomachean Ethics*, Aristotle explains that living a virtuous life is precisely what constitutes living a *good* human life, which is to say, human flourishing or happiness. The heart of his explanation is this: There are two fundamental truths about every natural thing ("natural" here simply refers to things not crafted by man). The first is that it has a given essence, called its "nature". An apple tree, for instance, has a nature; this is something shared by all apple trees that allows us to recognize an apple tree as an apple tree. The second truth is that each thing has a goal or state of flourishing called its "end". The end of the apple tree is to grow in good health to full stature and then produce well-formed apples. It is obvious that in all that an apple tree does, this is its goal or end; this is what it is "trying" to do. Anyone who knows apple trees can discern well enough their nature and their end.

Now, it is particularly in knowing the end or goal that

[3] *Apology* 39b.

one can judge between a *good* and a *bad* apple tree. A good apple tree is one that either has achieved, or is achieving, the goal of all apple trees. A bad apple tree is one that is not. Further, those things that are conducive to or lead to an apple tree's health and production of fruit are said to be "good" for apple trees. Similarly, what injures the tree's health and production of fruit is said to be "bad" for apple trees.

It is worth noting that sometimes the goodness or badness of something for the tree is not always immediately apparent. In other words, what *appears* at first to be bad might in reality be good, or vice versa. For example, the pruning of an apple tree, which seems at first to damage it, ultimately is very conducive to its healthy growth.

Now, though human nature is much more complex and noble than the nature of a tree, the same basic truths apply. There is a natural flourishing for man, and his actions can be judged as good or bad in terms of this end. What is the end of man? Aristotle answers that it is a life of complete virtue.

This point must be appreciated. Aristotle is not only saying that if one is to live well, virtue is necessary. He is saying that to live the whole range of virtues *is* to live well. And thus, since to live virtuously is the goal or end of human life, all other things in human life are ultimately judged as good or bad by their relation to virtue. What is conducive to virtue is good for a person; what hinders virtue is bad for a person. Since ethics is all about living a good or happy human life, and a good or happy human life is a life of virtue, therefore, the bulk of Aristotle's *Nicomachean Ethics* is about virtues: the kinds of virtue, how we develop them, and so forth.

But first we must step back and ask, Just what is a virtue?

Virtue is a *habit*, or a firm disposition to act in a certain kind of way. Experience shows that performing actions of a certain kind gives a person a sort of disposition or tendency to perform that kind of action again. This is why we practice various actions—such as playing the piano or swinging an ax—knowing that performing actions over and over again makes it progressively easier to do them. We also know how important it is to practice correctly, for the way we do the actions now is the way we will tend to keep doing them. Aristotle would put it this way: performing good actions, such as giving help to those in need, develops a habit of doing those good actions, while performing bad actions, such as stealing or lying, develops a habit of doing those bad actions.

The simplest definition of virtue, then, is that it is a good habit. We should note, though, that "habit" here refers to a disposition in the soul, not just a learned bodily behavior, such as swinging an ax. These firm dispositions—sometimes I call them "grooves in the soul"—are profound characteristics that determine in a unique way *who we are*. To say that a man is a man of courage says much. It says something important not only about how he acts but also about who and what he is.

The *Catechism of the Catholic Church* (*CCC*) treats of the virtues known as cardinal virtues, giving definitions that are fundamentally compatible with Aristotle's. Justice is "the moral virtue that consists in the constant firm will to give their due to God and neighbor" (1807). For an example of justice, we can think of the employer who always pays his employees a living wage, even when he could get away with giving less. Fortitude, or courage, is "the moral virtue that ensures firmness in difficulties and constancy in the pursuit of the good" (1808). An example is a young mother whose husband has left her, who perseveres in fidelity to her marriage (assuming that it was a valid marriage) and to the proper raising of her children. And temperance is "the moral virtue that moderates the attraction of pleasures and provides balance in the use of created goods" (1809). An example is the young person who disciplines the sexual desire and is committed to waiting for marriage. In each instance the virtue is a firm disposition or inclination in the soul. Therefore, having a virtue, a good habit, means being firmly disposed to perform good actions, and to perform them with ease and even joy. On the other hand, having a vice, or a bad habit, means being disposed to perform bad actions.

Having virtues or vices is at the center of a person's moral character. To see this, we must appreciate that most of our actions spring from our habits. Throughout the day, a person acts and reacts primarily through established habits of acting and reacting. Consider yourself in the following situation. A five-dollar bill drops from the pocket of a person walking in front of you on a crowded street. After you pick it up, what will you do? You will most likely do what you have done in similar situations before. It would be very unusual, for instance, for a person who habitually returns property to its rightful owner (this is a part of justice) to decide at that moment, "Today, I'm going to keep this for myself!" Similarly, a habitual thief (who practices a form of injustice) will almost surely keep the five-dollar bill, considering today his lucky day. How does a person respond in a situation of danger or a situation of personal provocation? Does that person respond with courage and good temper or with cowardice and unbridled anger? The response will tend to be from habit: virtue or vice.

Virtuous persons are those who, through a desire to do

what is good and right, have disciplined themselves and consistently direct their appetites or desires. These persons have gotten to the point where virtuous actions come very naturally, *because these actions are truly what they most want to do.* This is the profound beauty of virtue: being good really becomes your own way of being. Good thoughts and actions flow from your deepest self; they flow from who you are. This might be hard for us to imagine because we are still far from being truly virtuous.

Consider Mother Teresa of Calcutta. Her attitudes and actions toward the needy flowed from deep within her; they were an expression of her deepest desires, her truest self. And it showed. Those whom she helped saw that she was more than a woman who just happened to help the poor. It is said that, one day, a dying man who was not Christian asked her, "Is Jesus like you?" She said, "No. But I try to be like him." He responded, "Then I want to be a Christian too."

Here we should note that, for a Christian, the life of virtue is raised to a larger context—that of serving and being transformed in the Lord. The virtues of which Aristotle speaks all take on a deeper meaning and importance when we realize that they are aspects of sanctification, of becoming more Christlike.

It should now be a little clearer why Aristotle insists that *to be virtuous is to be happy.* Virtuous persons are those who consistently act from a desire for what is truly good and noble. These persons have largely overcome evil desires, since they love things according to their true worth. They do the right things *and* enjoy doing them, since right things are what they most want to do. This is the natural fulfillment or flourishing of human nature. This is part of the greatness for which God has made us. He wants us to do the right things at all times and in all places. But more than this, he wants these actions to spring from our very core, from our own desire and love. Ultimately, he wants them to spring from love of him, and that is what it means to have the highest virtue of all—supernatural charity. Charity is a love for God, and also for neighbor, that should become the source and inspiration of all our actions. As a *supernatural* and theological virtue (like faith and hope), it can be acquired only with what Christians call sanctifying grace. Supernatural virtues are at the heart of the Christian's life. Though many of the examples of virtues in this book will be of natural virtues —the ones Aristotle talks about—we will never lose sight of the fact that Christians understand a life well lived, or a virtuous life, as including all the virtues, especially the theological virtues of faith, hope, and charity. We will discuss charity at some length in the last chapter.

Aristotle makes a helpful distinction between two kinds of virtue. He divides them into "moral virtues" and "intellectual virtues". We can characterize moral virtues as the virtues related to how we desire and act. Intellectual virtues are virtues of the strictly intellectual, or knowing, power of man. We can characterize them as virtues of how we think or understand. The word "virtue" is often used as synonymous with "moral virtue", examples of which are justice, courage, and temperance. Yet there are also several intellectual virtues, the most important being wisdom, which is often forgotten when we think of virtue. For instance, we might refer to a person as "virtuous *and* wise". In this usage, "virtuous" is meant as synonymous with "morally virtuous". This usage is not a problem; there is a reason for it that we need not go into. Yet we should take note of this point, for when we consider the good life as the "life of virtue", while we focus on moral virtue, we must not forget the intellectual virtues—particularly wisdom. And again, for Christians, there are the theological virtues, which oversee all the virtues, as well as supernatural versions of the natural virtues that are infused with grace.

The moral virtues, again, are all about directing our desires toward what is truly good, so that what is truly good is, more and more, all that we really want. Someone might reasonably comment: "I would like to desire what is good, but I find myself desiring bad things. So I do what I can: I try to say no to my desires for bad things, and I try to force myself to do what I know is right. Isn't this enough? And besides, what more can I do?" This is very important. This person should be commended for these efforts. Yet what this person needs to see is that we can do more, even on the natural level, as understood by Aristotle. Above and beyond doing good actions, we can and should try to *reform our desires, changing them for the better.* For example, in the realm of justice, our goal should not simply be always to give what is due to God and neighbor; it should be to do so out of a profound desire for justice, and ultimately out of love of God (again, charity). In the realm of almsgiving, the goal should be to give to the service of God, or to the needy, not merely out of a sense of duty, but out of a real desire to serve God and others. Can there be any doubt that this is how the widow whom Jesus praised in the Gospel gave her offering (see Mk 12:41–44)?

But what can a person do to reform, or change, his desires? For Christians, grace will play the central role in the reform of our wants and desires. The great Saint Augustine (354–430) can be a role model for all of us. He wasted his early adult life in dissolute living, indulging his sexual appetite, among other things. When he heard God's call, and determined to answer it, he realized that two things were required for him to change his life: unceasing prayer and unceasing effort to change his habits.

This is an excellent twofold approach that we can imitate. We should first of all constantly pray to God to help us reform or change our desires. Saint Augustine speaks of the desire that should be at the center of our hearts: the desire for God himself. He thanks God for having strengthened in him this desire:

> Hear my prayer, O Lord; let not my soul fail under Thy discipline, nor let me fail in uttering to Thee Thy mercies: by them Thou hast drawn me out of all my most evil ways, that I should find more delight in Thee than in all the temptations I once ran after, and should love Thee more intensely, and lay hold upon Thy hand with all my heart's strength, and be delivered from every temptation unto the end.[4]

Would Our Lord Jesus ever resist the person who prays, "Strengthen my desire for you *and* my desire for those other things that you want me to desire"?

We must take other steps in addition to prayer to root out bad desires and to cultivate good ones. The main way to root out the bad ones is to starve them. This involves, for instance, avoiding persons and occasions (such as certain movies or certain social gatherings) that draw us into indulging bad desires, such as desires for gossip or drunkenness, lying, or sexual indulgence. The key here is to be willing just to say no.

But while we are saying no to bad desires, we should be saying yes to good ones. In other words, we *strive to replace bad desires with good ones*. Where there is a desire for injustice, cultivate a desire for justice. Where there is a desire

---

[4] *Confessions* 1, 15.

for sexual misconduct, cultivate a desire for pure love and personal communion. Where there is cowardice, or an unwillingness to endure pain in pursuit of or in defense of some good, cultivate a greater love of the good to be sought or defended. The main way to cultivate good desires is to *expose ourselves to the goodness and beauty of truly good things*. Experience of what is good tends to evoke a desire for it. Many who do not desire virtue have had little or no experience, firsthand or otherwise, of the profound nobility and beauty of virtue. Perhaps we can taste the beginnings of this in our own lives. The nobility of virtue can also be experienced by turning to virtuous persons—either in person, or in writing or art. We should seek to expose ourselves to virtue in each of these contexts. But the most powerful experience of virtue in another person is usually the experience of virtue in a friend.

Now we are ready to start to think about friendship.[5]

The Wisdom of the Ancients on Friendship

My students in ethics always get a surprise as we approach the end of Aristotle's *Nicomachean Ethics*. Aristotle devotes to friendship two whole chapters (or books, 8 and 9), more than he devotes to any other topic or specific virtue. Knowing that he owes some explanation for spending so much time on friendship, Aristotle gets right to the heart of the matter as he opens book 8: "After what we have said, a discussion of friendship would naturally follow, since it is a virtue or implies virtue, and is besides most necessary with

---

[5] For a fuller consideration of the nature of virtue see the resources at the end of this book.

a view to living. For without friends no one would choose to live, though he had all other goods."[6]

Even if you had *all* other goods, you would *never* choose to live without friends. Is Aristotle simply making the obvious point that friends are good and everyone wants them? Clearly, he is saying this; but there is more. By the end of book 9, Aristotle has made clear that living in true friendship is equivalent to human happiness. This bears repeating: for Aristotle, to live in true friendship is to live the good life, to be happy. But did we not just say that to be virtuous is to be happy? Yes. One of our central themes will be to understand how being virtuous and being a true friend are necessarily connected with each other. Indeed, they are practically the same thing.

Here someone might reasonably pose a big question. Even if this is what Aristotle thought, does he not, as a pagan, miss certain important truths held by Christianity? This is an important question. Divine revelation indeed reveals truths that substantially alter the pagan worldview. But here we must keep our heads and not throw the baby out with the bath water. Saint Thomas Aquinas, a thirteenth-century Dominican priest generally considered to be one of the greatest of theologians, is convinced that much of what the philosopher Aristotle teaches is simply what human reason can see about reality without the aid of revelation in the Old and New Testaments. Saint Thomas insists that what reason truly sees is never *contradicted* by divine revelation, even while it is surpassed by divine revelation. God gave us reason, and he intends that we use it to understand ourselves and the world around us. What God reveals to us in the Old and New

---

[6] *Nicomachean Ethics* 1155a1–3.

Testaments does not cast aside, but rather builds upon, what our reason can see without divine revelation. This is why, in striving to understand and express complex theological issues, Saint Thomas never hesitated to turn to the wisdom of the ancient philosophers.

Does divine revelation, then, fundamentally alter Aristotle's understanding of virtue and friendship? We will have a more sufficient answer in the final chapter of this book. For now, we can give a preliminary answer. Christians know that above the natural virtues of which Aristotle speaks there are *supernatural* virtues. They also know that the ultimate end, or goal, of the human person is to enjoy *friendship* with God in heaven. According to Saint Thomas, the virtue of charity, which is a supernatural virtue and the perfection of the spiritual life, is defined in terms of friendship with God. It seems, then, that *far from giving us cause to reject it, divine revelation gives us new impetus to try to understand Aristotle's notion of friendship.* Understanding his notion of friendship will be a great help in our understanding the Christian life.

Christians seem to have two extra motives for examining *human* friendship (beyond the importance it has in itself), so well understood by Aristotle. First, an understanding of human friendship enhances our understanding of friendship with God. Indeed, if we do not understand true human friendship, we will be hampered in understanding friendship with God. Second, and even more pressing, human friendship is the natural preparation for entering into friendship with God.

Consider the following. In his last heart-to-heart talk with the apostles, we find Christ saying these words:

> This is my commandment, that you love one another as I have loved you. Greater love has no man than this, that a

man lay down his life for his friends. You are my friends if you do what I command you. No longer do I call you servants, for the servant does not know what his master is doing; but I have called you friends, for all that I have heard from my Father I have made known to you. (Jn 15:12–15)

Christ reveals that he, the Lord of all, intends friendship with his creatures. What a stunning revelation! But if we do not have some knowledge and experience of true friendship, what will this revelation mean to us? What does a call to friendship with Christ *mean*? It means something very specific and profound.

It helps to begin by trying to understand human friendship. It is clearly part of God's providential plan that, for the most part, humans will first discover and exercise friendship with other human persons. This means that what we know of human friendship, and, more importantly, how we live out human friendship, are a critical preparation for the most important relationship in our lives: friendship with God. To gain insight into friendship, in this book we will turn to what wise and virtuous persons—particularly Aristotle, Saint Thomas Aquinas, and Saint Aelred of Rievaulx —have discovered from their experience of human friendship.

Yet one might ask: "Is it really necessary to *study* the nature of friendship? Since friendship is natural to people, can't we count on it just to happen through the normal course of events, without special effort?" Here I answer with a firm denial. I grant that people have a strong desire for friendship, and even an innate sense of friendship, and these are good indications of how natural our need is. But true friendship does not simply happen. Ongoing, intentional effort is needed. True friendship is an *art*, and a habit, that must be developed through practice. Although the *beginnings* of it do sometimes just "happen", or fall into place, true friendship is the result of intentional striving. Mozart had the *beginnings* of musical greatness by natural endowment and the surroundings of his upbringing. Yet his excellence in composition was the fruit of studied, persistent effort. Friendship, like great music, is a masterpiece; it happens because persons know what they want and thus develop the "skills"—especially the virtues —necessary to achieve their great goal.

It becomes clear now why an explicit *study* of the nature of friendship is very helpful in building true friendships. Friendship, as a kind of masterpiece, must be developed in a specific way. The more we understand the nature of that for which we are striving, the better we can strive for and attain it. Would anyone consider pursuing greatness as a composer without first studying principles of composition? And how much more important, and profound, is friendship!

Although I have suggested that our call to friendship with God provides the greatest motive to examine human friendship, it is not the only motive. Bearing in mind Aristotle's point that to live out true friendship is to live the good life, we should not be surprised (although many will be) that friendship is essentially connected with all the most important things in life. In examining different aspects of friendship, this book will touch on several of these important things.

Here is a brief overview of this book. Chapter 2 distinguishes between the kinds of friendship and focuses on the nature of the most important kind, virtuous friendship. Chapter 3 argues that friendship is a major determinant of a person's self-image and also a major determinant of who that person really is. Chapter 4 considers how, through friendship, a person forms habits—virtues or vices—and thus develops character for better or for worse. Chapter 5 considers how friendship is more than a private matter between friends and how a good civil society both requires virtuous friendships among citizens and, at the same time, plays an important role in fostering good friendships. Chapter 6 turns to the great wisdom of Saint Aelred for practical steps in discerning with whom to pursue friendship and how to test it in its early stages. Chapter 7 argues that virtuous friendships help ensure that young men and women can and will engage in timely and honorable courtship and that they will be prepared for marriage. Chapter 8 examines the issue of being friends in a different yet very important sense, with parents, teachers, and mentors. And finally, chapter 9 examines friendship with God as the root of divine and natural law, the perfection of the spiritual life, and the very end, or goal, of human life.

Questions for Discussion

1. What does Socrates mean when he says, "The most important thing is not life, but the good life?"

2. What are virtues, and why are they so important in life?

3. Why is it helpful to *study* friendship?

Questions for Personal Reflection

1. Sirach 6:15 says: "There is nothing so precious as a faithful friend, and no scales can measure his excellence." Do I hold friendship (not simply the person who is a friend, but friendship with this person) to be among the most precious things in my life—indeed, something whose excellence is beyond measure?

2. Do I *act* as though friendship is that precious? How can others see in my actions that I hold friendship to be that precious?

3. How often do I think about what friendship is and how to develop it?

2

Friendship and Its Kinds

For there is a friend who is such at his own convenience,
but will not stand by you in your day of trouble. . . .
A faithful friend is a sturdy shelter: he that has found one
has found a treasure.

— Sirach 6:8, 14

What is friendship? Before answering this question, we must
consider the question itself. It is always helpful to understand what is being asked before answering a question! In
one of the famous Platonic dialogues, Socrates asks a man
named Euthyphro to answer the question "What is piety?"
Euthyphro, who has a reputation for wisdom in religious
matters, answers the question with haste and confidence. He
answers by giving an example of a pious action. Socrates explains to Euthyphro that to give an example of something,
while not irrelevant, is not the same as to answer the question "What is it?" "Bear in mind then", he says, "that I did
not bid you tell me one or two of the many pious actions but
the form itself that makes all pious actions pious."[1] There
is some form, or we can say nature or essence, that all pious
actions have in common. To point to that nature is truly to
answer the question "What is piety?" Now, it is in a good
definition that we express our understanding of what a thing
is, or the nature of a thing. And, as Euthyphro learns in the

[1] *Euthyphro* 6d.

rest of the dialogue, it is much easier to point to an example than to give a good definition.

But perhaps the ability to point to examples is all we need. Do we really need a definition? The Euthyphro dialogue contains the answer to this question. It becomes clear that an inability to give a good definition of piety casts doubt upon the ability to recognize what is or is not an example of piety. How can Euthyphro be sure that a particular action is pious if he is not quite sure *what piety is*?

What have we learned about our question "What is friendship?" In asking this question, we are seeking the nature of friendship, or just what it is that makes a relationship a friendship. If we can answer this question, then we *know* that we can recognize which relationships are, and which are not, friendships. This is not an easy task. Let us turn to the wise for help.

Friendship in General

As Aristotle begins his consideration of friendship in the *Nicomachean Ethics*, he takes it as a given that friendship essentially involves love or affection for some object. Of course, there are many instances of love or affection for some object that are not instances of friendship. In which instances of affection would we say that there is a friendship?

Aristotle points to three characteristics that distinguish a friend from other objects of affection. First, among objects of affection, there are only certain ones *toward which* or *for which* you can have goodwill. To have goodwill for something means to wish something well. Aristotle gives the example of wine. One might have affection for wine, but one does not wish wine well; one would not say to it,

"I hope all is going well for you." Second, among objects of goodwill, only certain ones reciprocate, or return, goodwill. For instance, though one can wish a baby well, a baby cannot reciprocate goodwill. Similarly, I can have goodwill toward a neighbor who is capable of returning goodwill but who, in fact, does not. Third, among situations of reciprocal goodwill, there is not always mutual recognition of the goodwill. For instance, my neighbor and I might have some kind of goodwill for each other, but we might not realize that the other returns it.

These points lead to a commonsense, general characterization of friendship. Aristotle concludes: "To be friends, then, they must be mutually recognized as bearing goodwill and wishing well to each other."[2] Aristotle has led his reader to be able to formulate a *general definition of friendship*: it is a mutually recognized relationship of goodwill that occurs between human persons. But just what does it mean to have goodwill for another? At this point, Aristotle has left this vague because there are, in fact, different kinds of friendships, depending on the kind of "goodwill" or "wishing well" that is present. This makes sense because, if there are different kinds of friendship, then the characterization of friendship itself must be general enough to include the various kinds. Aristotle next distinguishes between different kinds of friendship according to the kind of "good" that is willed in each case. A further point we will see as we proceed is that the goodwill in friendship is always lived out in some way; it is not just a dormant wishing.

[2] *Nicomachean Ethics* 1156a3–5.

Basic Kinds of Friendship

Aristotle distinguishes three objects of affection or love: the pleasant, the useful, and the honorable good or the virtuous good. Each of these can be the "good" that is mutually willed in a friendship, so there are three kinds of friendship that correspond to these three goods. We can call them the "pleasant friendship", the "useful friendship", and the "virtuous friendship". Let us note from the start that these are *not* mutually exclusive kinds; they are basic types. As we proceed, we will see how helpful it is to distinguish these types.

In the pleasant friendship, two people find each other's company to be pleasant. This friendship is basically about having a good time together. What each sees and values in the other is that the other is the cause of some pleasure for himself. "Pleasure" here refers especially to the level of what appeals to the senses. This friendship is particularly found among young people. Since young people tend to focus more on pleasure, they tend to develop relationships based on it. A good example of this is two college students who have a friendship primarily because they socialize together.

In the useful friendship, each person receives some benefit from the presence or actions of the other, and this is the basis for the relationship. Many business relationships are useful friendships when each person, as a matter of course, provides for the needs of the other. Another example is a relationship between two high school students, in which one regularly helps the other study in exchange for favors of some other kind.

The key divide between the kinds of friendship is between the first two kinds on the one hand, and virtuous friendship on the other. The best way to introduce the virtuous friendship is to stop and consider what is shared by the first two kinds. The most important shared characteristic is, in fact, what is *not* there, what is absent. In the pleasant friendship and the useful friendship, the love or goodwill between the friends that grounds the relationship is neither (a) for the other's sake nor (b) because of who the other is in himself.

Let us consider (a). In the first two kinds of friendship, each person tends to focus on what can be derived from the relationship: some good received from the other person, either pleasure or utility. The basis of the relationship is not a concern about the well-being of the other. This does not contradict Aristotle's assertion that in all friendships there is some good willed *to the other*, because the person does want to be pleasant or useful to the other. But the person wants this ultimately so that the other will be pleasant or useful in return. The relationship is most of all based on what each gets from the other.

Now, these relationships are not simply an exercise in selfishness—though they could be. The point is more nuanced. Consider the business relationship referred to above. Between these two men there could well be general good feelings and some real well-wishing, yet a close look at the relationship shows that it is primarily about utility. The same might be said for those in a friendship of pleasure. Perhaps they have a genuine liking for each other, and this relationship really could become something more. But again, the reality now is a relationship rooted in enjoying each other's company, and not much more.

As regards (b), when the friends are not primarily loved because of who they are in themselves, what we find is that each person focuses on what is "incidental" to the other, as opposed to seeing the other for who he is. Our business relationship is not based on the "inner persons" of those involved, such as the merchant and the supplier. It is based on the reality that the supplier is useful to the merchant, and vice versa. Note that the supplier's usefulness to the merchant and the merchant's usefulness to the supplier are not defining features of who they are as persons. To know that supplier Jane is a woman who can reliably supply sellable goods is, in fact, to know very little about Jane. And to know that merchant Tom is an outstanding salesman of those goods is to know very little about Tom. A relationship based on these characteristics is not really based on the persons in themselves. Similarly, in a pleasant friendship, a person's pleasantness, or the ability to bring about a good time, is not at the heart of who the person is. It is for this reason that we say that, in these friendships, persons are not loved because of who they are in themselves, but rather because of something incidental, something that they just happen to be or do.

Does this mean that the first two kinds of friendship are bad and should be avoided? The answer is a definite no. These kinds of friendship are natural, and *they have their place in everyone's life*. What is very important, however, is to recognize these for what they are, and what they are not. We also need to learn to live them well. Even though a relationship is not *based on* a love of the other for who he is, this friendship can still be lived with respect and integrity. When Aristotle calls them "incidental friendships", he means that they are not friendships in the full and most important sense. They can be called friendships because in a limited way they fit the general definition above, but they fall short of what full or true friendship is all about. Making this distinction is a big step toward understanding the most important kind of friendship.

Most of us have had a relationship that we thought was a friendship but then discovered that in some important sense it was not. What is it that we discovered? Usually it is one of the two things just mentioned regarding the pleasant or useful friendships. I have often heard people say, "He wasn't really looking out for *my* good after all", or "She just didn't appreciate me for *who I am*." We will consider more in the next chapter why this can be such a devastating experience. The problem here is usually that one or both persons expected the kind of real communion, or meeting of souls, that comes only in a full friendship, or a virtuous friendship, as Aristotle calls it. And it turns out that there wasn't one, but something much more like a pleasant friendship or a useful friendship.

So what is virtuous friendship?

Friendship in the Full Sense: Virtuous Friendship

Aristotle says: "Now those who wish well to their friends for their own [the others'] sake are most truly friends; for they do this by reason of their own [the others'] nature and not incidentally."[3] Here is the flip side of what was said about the first two kinds of friendship. In a virtuous friendship, the friends each love the other (a) for the other's sake and (b) because of who the other is in himself—that is, not because of something incidental to him. The first point is very simple but of the utmost significance. True friends (and by "true" here I mean in the full sense, this third sense) are those who love the other in the sense of wanting what is best for him. They are able to transcend simply looking out for their own advantage. Here, one's desire, extending beyond

[3] Ibid., 1156b9–10.

private fulfillment, is for the fulfillment, the flourishing, of the friend.

The second point, that the friends see each other for who each is, is closely linked to the first. How can someone really desire my good if that person sees me *only* as a good source of entertainment or as a productive partner? I may be socially adept and have great prowess in the marketplace, but only the person who sees beyond that, to what is deep inside of me, and cares, can be my true friend.

But why does Aristotle call this "virtuous friendship"? We have seen that friendships are distinguished according to the good that is willed. Again, in the pleasant friendship, pleasure is willed in some sense *to* the other person, but primarily because pleasure returns to the first person. Here, pleasure is not only willed or desired as something still to be achieved more and more, but it is also the *basis* of the relationship because it is what got the relationship started. The friendship began when two people, such as the two college students, found themselves enjoying the same things and enjoying each other.

Now we can begin to see the profundity of Aristotle's notion of full friendship. Full friendship is that relationship of mutual goodwill that is based on the virtue, or true goodness, of two persons. It is *based on* virtue because this kind of relationship can really get going only when each person, at least to some extent, is already virtuous. It is also based on virtue inasmuch as virtue or goodness is the main thing that is willed, desired, and sought in the relationship. What does a true friend want most of all? The virtue of his friend: that it be, and increase! This fits beautifully with the insight that a friend wants what is best for his friend. As discussed earlier, virtue is always what is best for a person, period.

But is it true that a person must already be virtuous in

order to have true friendship? Aristotle is insistent on this point, though with some nuance. Of this third and most important kind of friendship, Aristotle says that it "is the friendship of men who are good, and alike in virtue".[4] True friendship requires that a person already be, to some real extent, virtuous. We might put it like this: to the extent that a person is truly intent on virtue, and only to that extent, can that person have a share in true friendship. In other words, one need not be perfectly virtuous in order to have a true friendship; yet at the same time, *falling short in virtue implies a falling short in achieving full friendship*. Why is this so?

It is the virtuous person, to the extent that he is virtuous, who really has the ability to do what true friends do together, starting with willing and pursuing the true good of another person. To say to another person, "I want what is best for you" is one thing. To *mean it* is another. And to be able to *help him achieve it* is yet another. Anyone can say it. It takes some virtue to mean it. It takes more virtue truly to do it.

Recall our example of Susan and Mary. Mary would undoubtedly declare that she wants what is best for Susan. Yet, when it comes to a situation such as the car wreck, Mary's inability to want what is best for Susan comes to the fore.

Allow me to qualify these assertions through explanation. Let us consider first the virtuous person and then the unvirtuous person. The virtuous person has become virtuous through grace and much effort. This person habitually deliberates about (that is, rationally considers) what constitutes a *good* life, *and* desires and acts in accordance with what he has seen to be truly good. Through habitually choosing what is truly good, especially the higher goods of the soul, this

---

[4] Ibid., 1156b6.

person is singularly capable of recognizing true goodness in other persons and of choosing that good over lesser goods, such as pleasure and utility. It is precisely this person who is able to transcend selfish desire and truly to will and act for the good of the other. This is an amazing moment, a wonderful feat. This person, striving to center life on what is truly good, as opposed to self-gratification, is thus capable of a fundamentally unselfish, other-centered stance. Further, this person knows from experience what is involved in pursuing the virtuous life and, through this familiarity, is just the one to help another along the same way.

What about the unvirtuous—in other words, all of us, to the extent that we lack virtue? Very few persons are completely self-centered. At least some who have not grown in virtue are surely still capable of some goodwill toward others. A person might say, "I want what is best for you" and mean it, as regards, for instance, his family, as people usually have some real affection for their family members. The person might also mean it as regards people with whom he has grown up or people in his group of close friends. But a close and honest examination reveals two major reasons why a lack of virtue implies a weakness or even paralysis in living out such relationships, especially as regards true friendship. First, lacking virtue goes hand in hand with putting an unhealthy priority on self—i.e., with some degree of selfishness. Second, lacking virtue implies an inability really to help others become happy.

Let us consider the problem of being selfish—the bane of true friendship. We noted above that virtuous persons are those who have centered their lives not on selfish desires but on the higher, or true, human good, according to what right reason discerns. Is this not a fundamental goal in raising children? Parents train children to use their reason to discern what is truly good in life, what is most important, and how to desire and act in accord with it. This requires effort on the part of parents *and* children. It requires effort because, in order to live a good life, one must form virtues of thought, desire, and action that are often contrary to some inclinations of our fallen nature. The sure sign of an unformed teenager, or an immature adult, is a habitual inability or unwillingness to set aside selfish desires for the sake of higher goods. It is the unvirtuous person, then, who is largely incapable of a true other-centered attitude, a true willing of the good of the other for the other's sake, which is the heart of friendship. This becomes more apparent the more we realize that friendships demand a willingness to sacrifice and give of self—something that experience makes eminently clear.

The second reason that those who lack virtue are paralyzed as regards full friendship is their inability to help others to become truly happy. A main topic in the fourth chapter will be how friends help one another to grow in virtue and thus in happiness. One who is not growing in virtue has either not discerned what the truly good life is or in some way lacks the will to pursue it. In either case, this person is unable to help others to grow in virtue. But helping another to grow in virtue is essential to friendship. It is here that the tragedy of not being virtuous, or not living the truly good life, starts to become clear. Deep in our hearts, we all desire not only to be happy, but also to help others to be happy and to be happy together with them. The unvirtuous person is frustrated on all counts. Let us be clear on this: all of us, to the extent that we fail in virtue, are frustrated on all these counts. This should become more and more evident as we proceed.

Let us consider another example in which the lack of

virtue ruins the possibility of true friendship. A young man named James is living an unchaste lifestyle. He is a nice young man and a good college student. But, for him, premarital sex is a reasonable option, as long as both persons act voluntarily. James enjoys spending time with his dorm mate Patrick and wants to have a friendship with him. But we have seen that true friendship is about persons pursuing the good life together. Now, one of the main moral challenges that all young men must face is the challenge to control sexual desires. Since James is fundamentally failing in this area—in other words, he is not willing to control his desires (which is very different from a young man's being fundamentally in control of his desires, even though he still occasionally fails in certain ways)—he cannot truly pursue the good life with Patrick. Patrick cannot turn to him and count on him for support in his own struggles in this area. On that Saturday when Patrick needs the support of a true friend as he makes his evening plans, James is not going to be there for him.

One objection that is often raised against the claim that virtue is necessary for friendship is this: How can any of us really be friends, since we are so far from perfection in virtue? This is a critical point. I said above that to the extent that a person is virtuous, and only to that extent, can that person have a share in true friendship. Likewise, to the extent that a person fails in virtue, that person lacks the capacity for true friendship. Thus, there are degrees of capability for true friendship. Indeed, there is no upper limit, as there is always room to grow in virtue and thus in friendship. But there must be a bottom limit, below which there is no real capability for true friendship. I would put it this way: the minimum requirement for being capable of true friendship is that a person is dedicated to the pursuit of virtue, or, for

Christians, we can broaden this to say holiness, making it the focus of life.

We would do well to bear in mind that Aristotle held that true friendships are rare, especially for this reason: virtuous persons are rare. But this is not a reason for despair. Rather, we press onward, with hope, in pursuit of friendship, since "he that has found one has found a treasure" (Sir 6:15) and "with God all things are possible" (Mt 19:26). Here we should note that the great Saint Aelred, whose writings we will examine later, rejoices that Christians know to beg God for the grace to achieve the true friendship that, naturally speaking, is so difficult to achieve.

A Few More Points about Virtuous Friendship

Virtuous friendship is the focus of this book, because it is this friendship that most answers to the name of "true friendship". There is much more to say about this kind of friendship, but let us begin here with a few more points about it.

Although Aristotle distinguishes between pleasant friendship, useful friendship, and virtuous friendship, he is careful to point out that virtuous friendships have *all* these qualities: pleasure, usefulness, and the virtuous good. Persons who have virtuous or full friendship find each other most pleasant and most useful. Indeed, what or who is more pleasant or useful in the most important sense than the virtuous person? For this reason, Aristotle proceeds to assert that virtuous friendships are the most stable, long-lasting, and noble of friendships.

Pleasant or useful friendships, on the other hand, tend to be short-lived. Again, unlike the friendship that is based on who the persons are in themselves, these friendships are based on pleasantness or utility. The pleasantness and utility of a person can easily change, and thus, these relationships come and go more easily. This is particularly apparent in young people, whose friendships tend to be pleasant friendships. The person whom a nine-year-old, or even a teenager, finds pleasant can change rather easily. And those college students who enjoy only socializing together can find that their relationship basically ends when the social scene changes. On the other hand, virtuous friendship is built on rock, grounded in who the persons are, which, in virtuous souls, is an especially enduring reality.

Aristotle expresses the unique and beautiful nature of virtuous friendship with the notion of "another self". "But the good man feels toward his friend as toward himself, since his friend is another self."[5] Think of this. One looks upon another person as though that other were one's very self! This is the height of other-centeredness. For the friend says to the friend: "It is as important to me that you are happy as that I am happy. When you flourish, when you are blessed, I rejoice with you, for it is as though it is my flourishing and blessedness. When you fail or suffer, I fail and suffer. All that you enjoy or endure, we enjoy or endure together." The great story in Scripture of the friendship between David and Jonathan illustrates this point. Scripture records that "the soul of Jonathan was knit to the soul of David, and Jonathan loved him as his own soul" (1 Sam 18:1).

Does this mean that friends come to have precisely the same likes and dislikes? Though in some profound sense the answer is yes (which we will return to later), we can say no. Friends retain their individual likes and dislikes as

---

[5] Ibid., 1170b5.

regards many things. But here is an opportunity to observe the unique unifying nature of friendship. Suppose a man loves to hike in the great outdoors. He does not expect all his true friends to love hiking too. There is, nevertheless, a sense in which any true friend of his will come to love it. He will love it *through* him, or *in* his loving it. The friend may never go hiking himself, but he loves *his friend's going hiking*, simply because, as another self, he shares in his loves.

We noted that Aristotle warns us that virtuous friendships are rare, particularly because virtuous persons are rare. Yet another reason these relationships are rare is that they take time and a sustained, conscious effort to form. True friendship always requires really knowing the other person. We do well to ask ourselves: How many people really know who I am? Indeed, we might even ask: Do *I* really know who I am? Here we are in deep waters. The realities of true friendship and what it requires always connect to the deepest aspects of human life. I can strive more and more to become myself, to discover who I am, and to learn how to see others for who they are. Then, in any case, I will be more ready to get to know, and to be known by, the most important people in my life.

A Final Note about the Kinds of Friendship

The most important division between the kinds of friendship is the distinction between the first two kinds, pleasant and useful friendships, and the third kind, virtuous friendship. It is critical that we understand the nature of virtuous friendship. It is the living out of *this* friendship that, for Aristotle, is equivalent to the good life.

But do not worry if you find yourself wondering: Do I

really have any friends like that? We *should* wonder about that and then do all that we can to improve our situation. We noted earlier that Aristotle does not divide friendship into three mutually exclusive kinds. For instance, virtuous friendships usually have grown out of one of the first two kinds. This growth takes time. Often the growth gets only so far. This is because, as we have emphasized, growth in true friendship is limited by growth in virtue as well as by time and other extrinsic factors. Some friendships are somewhere in between. They have elements of virtuous friendship and of one or both of the other two. But this is not the same as Aristotle's point that virtuous friendship is also most pleasant and most useful. The "mixture" we are speaking of now is a weak or limited virtuous friendship; it is one that is not fully *based on* who the person really is and on virtue. The other person is not as fully "another self" as that person can and should be, if there is to be virtuous friendship.

We need to be aware that we are limited in pursuing full or true friendships. Even virtuous persons can have only a limited number of these friendships. We cannot seek true friendship with everyone around us! There are friendships that are not what we are calling true friendships that nonetheless can be real friendships. Aristotle points out that the very nature of human life, as lived in our bodies in time and space, puts limitations on our ability to share our lives with other people. Forming and living out three or two or even one virtuous friendship will be an arduous task and will require much of us. We should strive to be true to all of our friends and friendships, of whatever kind. In other words, we can act with integrity, being true to what we share with one another, be it little or great, be it a friendship of utility or pleasure or a virtuous friendship. Sometimes this will mean recognizing that, for various reasons, we cannot go any deeper with a certain person. Chapter 6 will examine this issue a little more.

Our main goal in this book is to understand the full friendship of virtue—what we are calling "true friendship"—so that we can make an explicit effort to grow in it. It is for this friendship especially that we naturally long. It is also this friendship that most prepares us for friendship with God, since our friendship with God should have the characteristics of virtuous friendship, raised to the highest degree.

Questions for Discussion

1. What is the main way to distinguish between the first two kinds of friendship (pleasant and useful friendships) and the third kind (true friendship)?

2. Why is it that one can be only as good a friend as one is virtuous? In other words, why is it that nonvirtuous persons cannot really be friends?

3. Are the first two kinds of friendship bad and to be avoided?

4. How does one of the first two kinds of friendship grow into true friendship?

5. What do we mean by saying that a friend is another self? Read 1 Samuel 18:1–4 on the friendship of David and Jonathan.

Questions for Personal Reflection

1. How well prepared am I for being a true friend? For instance, will my friends be inspired by my example to pursue virtue? Do I think in terms of living a good life *together with* my friends?

2. What can I do to improve my preparedness?

3. To what extent do I have true friendship in my life?

Exercise

Read the following texts about the greatest Old Testament friendship, that of David and Jonathan, in 1 Samuel 18:1–4; 20; 23:1–18; and 2 Samuel 1. Look for the characteristics of true friendship.

3

Friendship and Self-Image

A faithful friend is an elixir of life.

— Sirach 6:16

I will begin with an assertion that I will explain and defend in the next two chapters: your friends profoundly affect who you are. I intend this to mean two distinct things. First, friends are a major determinant of your self-image, and your self-image, or how you see yourself, is a major part of who you are. Second, it is with friends that you form habits and develop your character. This second point is the subject of the next chapter. In this chapter, the focus is on friendship and self-image.

Let us consider first what "self-image" means and then turn to consider the effect that others, especially friends, have on our self-image.

How You See Yourself

By "self-image" I mean, first of all, how one sees oneself. While this can, of course, refer to such things as seeing oneself as sociable or attractive, our main concern here is with a deeper level of seeing oneself. Do you see yourself as lovable? Do you see yourself as more than just a body? Do you see your life as worth living? Do you see yourself as belonging somewhere? Would you really be missed? Do you really have something to contribute to a community? Perhaps not every person poses these questions. Nevertheless, we know, at least in an unconscious way, that the answer to these questions is either yes or no and that our answer makes all the difference to who we are.

When I speak here of self-image, I don't mean image or appearance as opposed to reality. Rather, the point is that how we see ourselves should correspond to the truth of who we are and who we can be. Our age, tragically, is obsessed with image but encourages us to think of ourselves and others in terms of shallow and passing things, and it encourages us to focus more on how we appear to others than on who we really are. This makes it more difficult for us to know who we are and to see others for who they are.

Consider for a moment how important this matter is. Is not a young woman who sees moral character as central to who she is, and her life as full of meaning—regardless of what others think—a very different person from a young woman who is very concerned about what others think of her and at the same time doubts whether there is any point to her life? In an age in which the suicide rate has reached an unprecedented level, this matter takes on special significance.

But where does one's self-image come from? How is it developed? This is a very rich and complex question for which there are no simple answers. Nevertheless, there are a few basic points that seem to be beyond dispute. First, how *other people* see and treat a person is a major determining factor in that person's self-image. We can first consider the human person as a child. It is obvious that children do not come into the world with an understanding of the world and their place in it. Children are dependent on those around them to communicate, first by actions and later by words, a vision of themselves and the world. This is not to suggest that children are completely passive and play no role in the development of self-image. Certainly that is not the case. Children, however, fundamentally rely on others to "show them to themselves", to open their eyes to what it means to be a person—and to be this particular person!

As we mature, this dependence on others lessens, but it does not cease. Even mature adults depend on others to help them see themselves. For instance, to perceive clearly whether I am succeeding in my profession, I must depend on the judgment of others—not just any others, but others in my profession, particularly those who excel in it. Similarly, to know whether I am living up to my calling to be a good husband, I must turn to others—first my wife, and also to other husbands, perhaps ones more experienced than I am. And finally, to know whether I am succeeding in living a good life—indeed, especially here—I fundamentally depend on others.

Friends and Truly Seeing Yourself

We should note that certain persons are better suited than others to this role of helping a person see himself. When I ask myself how my game of tennis is or how good a plumber I am, I turn to the appropriate experts to help me form my self-image. But what about the most serious matters of all: Does my life have meaning? Am I living a good life? and so forth. Are there "experts" in these matters? Thank God there are. But who are these experts? The great Greek philosophers and Sacred Scripture use the same word to describe them: they are "the wise". They are the ones who grasp the meaning of life and know wherein lies true human greatness. As Socrates says, they understand what is most important in life and strive to live accordingly, which is to say that they strive to live virtuous lives.

But we must go further if we are to give an adequate answer to the question as to which others are best suited to helping us form a true self-image. What we saw in the last chapter about true friendship gives us the means to look more deeply into this. Let us recall the two characteristics of true friendship that distinguish it from the other kinds of friendship. First, the true friend sees the other as the other is in himself, which is to say that the person really understands the other. And second, the person seeks what is good for the friend; in other words, he loves the person *for his own sake*.

Now, surely the person who can most help us see ourselves is the one who is wise *and* who sees us for who we are, as individual persons. What we are saying, then, is this: a true friend is the one especially apt to help us form a true self-image. We must always bear in mind the essential connection between being a true friend and being a good person—that is, being virtuous. The true friend has the two main requirements for being the best one to help persons see themselves. Knowing the meaning of life, this person is dedicated to living out virtue *and* can see you as the individual person you are. The person can see because of having taken the time to get to know you—having broken bread together with you, as one expression says. It is probably to this person that you have entrusted your deepest secrets, hopes, and fears. And further, this person has the secret key to insight into your person: love for you.

There is a wonderful phrase about this in Latin: *Ubi amor, ibi oculus*—"Where there is love, there is the power to see" (literally, "an eye"). Does anyone know you the way the one who loves you knows you? There are many reasons why love produces insight into persons. We can consider a few of them. One who loves you is willing to take the time to get to know you as you really are. One interested in friendship of utility or pleasure might make an effort to get to know you, but since that person's primary interest is not *you*, he will not really have an "eye" for you yourself but will have an eye for other things.

This can also be seen in the related fact that one who loves you tends to have a "forgiving eye", an eye ready to look past your failings, while not ignoring them. Even the virtuous will sometimes fall short of what they can be. Really to know you, a person must be willing to look beyond your shortcomings. It is always a friend who is most forgiving. We can put it this way: the friend is willing and able to look beyond present shortcomings, to what you *can be*. This points to a beautiful insight into how God loves us.

This is a precious truth, that the "lover" (that is, one who truly loves me, as a true friend does) can most truly see me for who I am. But we can take this one step further. In a very profound sense, the true friend is especially capable of *showing me* truths about myself that I am incapable of seeing on my own or through others who do not love me. The first such truth is that I am lovable. Let us set aside for a moment the distinction between those who are striving for virtue and those who are not. Every human person is profoundly lovable. This is evident in the fact that all persons are created in the image and likeness of God and have been loved, in all their particularity, by God from all eternity. Jesus Christ is the Good Shepherd who gives His life for His sheep, each and every one of them.

Perhaps the most fundamental truth that human persons

need to see about themselves is the reality of God's love for them. But how does one come to know this love? Here we begin to enter a wonderful and mysterious aspect of divine providence. In the natural course of events, one normally discovers first that one is loved by other *human* persons. This is a natural foundation for the much greater discovery that one is loved by God himself. But what is meant by "foundation" here? Are we putting a limit on the grace of God by suggesting that being loved by human persons is in some sense a prerequisite for realizing God's love for us? Let us be clear on this important point: God's grace can overcome many obstacles. Thus, even a person who has never been loved by any other human person *can* come to realize God's love through God's grace. This truth, however, ought not to take away from our appreciation of another truth: that human love normally plays a central role in the discovery of God's love for us. According to the design of God himself, human persons usually discover their lovableness through human love, that is, other human persons loving them.

We can say that God has put a great burden upon the shoulders of humans, that they must, in a very real way, show one another their lovableness or show one another that they are loved by God. But what a precious burden this is! In God's providence human persons are the conduits, the instruments, God uses to show other human persons how much *he* loves them!

We were making the point that the true friend is the one who is especially capable of showing me truths about myself that I cannot see on my own. Of course, beyond showing me that I am lovable, the friend shows me specific ways in which I am lovable and also ways in which I am not lovable. The friend helps me to realize how and when I fall short of being the person I am called to be. For example, if Susan from our story had, through a momentary weakness, decided to lie to her father about the car wreck, a true friend would have responded by calling her back to her true self. "Susan, you are not the kind of person to do that!"

At this point a reasonable objection might be raised: Do I really need a true *friend* to help me see myself? Perhaps a loving family suffices for me to form a true self-image. Of course, all that has been said here should be taken as implying that the love experienced in the family is the natural and all-important starting point in the proper development of a true self-image. Experience, however, shows that family alone does not suffice. Even while still a child, and more and more so as one grows older, the person looks beyond the family to develop relationships.

Consider a girl who complains, "I don't have any friends." Her mother responds, "Well, sure you do. You have Daddy and me and your brother and sister." The girl retorts: "You all don't count. You *have* to like me—you're my family!"

It does no dishonor to the beauty and importance of family relationships to recognize that the girl has a point. It is very important that this girl appreciate the true love that her family has for her, but it is also important that she begin to experience true friendship outside the family. True friendship that comes from a peer outside the family provides a special completion or furthering of the love experienced inside the family. It has a special quality of gratuity—having been completely freely given—and a quality of objectivity that love from inside the family does not necessarily have.

This point is seen perhaps most clearly in one unique instance of true friendship: the true friendship that should develop between spouses. It is often the great joy of a happily married person to say to his spouse, "Only now am I most fully discovering who I am, through your love for me."

In summary, through true human friendship, we naturally come to see who we are, who we are called to be, and how we are doing in the journey of life. We come to have a sense of ourselves as lovable and worthy of the attention and affirmation of others. This is essential for understanding the place of friendship in human life and the importance of having true friends. One of the main causes of the tragedy of not having a true self-image is the lack of true friends.

Our treatment of friendship and self-image will not be complete unless we note that bad friends can create a bad self-image. We should first say a word about what a "bad friend" is. As noted earlier, it is not bad to have what Aristotle called friendships of pleasure or utility, as long as they are recognized for what they are. In other words, persons should realize that it is not with *these people* that they really share their lives in the most meaningful ways. There is a problem, however, when persons want a deep sharing but do not pursue the good life together. Another way of putting this is that a bad friend is one with whom you share your life but who draws you away from the truly good life, from virtue.

We will consider the influence of bad friends more in the next chapter, but here let us simply note their negative effect on self-image. It is the true friend who can see you for who you are and love you for your own sake. The bad friend cannot and does not do this. This person, then, is in no position to help you see yourself. Indeed, a bad friend often causes a person to have a skewed vision of himself as well as of the meaning of life. How does this happen? The bad friend does not pursue true goodness. As a result, this person tends to approve and encourage things in you that ought to be disapproved and discouraged, and he tends to disapprove things in you that ought to be approved. Think of the young man who praises his buddy for his ability to out-drink the other guys. "You're amazing—you're the best." Think of the partner who praises his friend for success in business while the latter is ignoring the needs of his family at home. Again, it is natural that we see ourselves through the eyes of our friends. In the case of the bad friend, we simply will not see ourselves in the right light.

Love for Those Who Do Not Pursue Virtue

I said above that when we consider the lovableness of *all* persons, we can set aside the distinction between those who are striving to live a good life and those who are not. Let us close this chapter with a little more consideration of this point. It would be fitting, although, sadly, it is often not the case, for all persons to have loving families as well as friends outside the family. Love from family and friends would take the form of appreciating persons in their particularity and wanting what is best for them. These two aspects are included in any true love for a person: an appreciation or affirmation *and* a wanting what is best. Thus, to say, "I love you" is to say, "I affirm you as good, and I want more good for you."

Again, all persons—even those who might be called evil persons—are worthy of love. God loves each and every one of us. In other words, he says to us: I affirm your goodness (which I have given you!), and I want you to grow in goodness. But *true love* (whether in God or in us) *does not affirm or approve of evil*.

What happens when one loves a person who pursues an evil path in life? One should have this disposition toward the other (but does not necessarily put it into words): "I affirm you as the particular person, the particular creature of God that you are, and I want what is best for you. But since you are not pursuing what is best for yourself, I cannot approve of how you are living. I want nothing more than for you to discover who you really are and what you are called to be. I want you to pursue the good life of virtue." Of course, one will do everything possible to aid the other in changing for the better. Prayer is always the first, and at times the only, recourse. "Lord, help us, and all those we love, to live the life that you call us to live."

We saw in the last chapter that true friendship requires that both friends pursue the virtuous life. Indeed, friendship is all about pursuing the good life *together*. In the preceding reflection, we see this point yet again. If the unvirtuous person who is truly loved by another person does not start to turn his life around, then he is, in effect, rejecting the offer of friendship from the other person. To the loving call to "be all that you are called to be" this person responds, "I want to live my life my own way." This leaves him in lonely, tragic isolation. Two persons pursuing virtue, on the other hand, can be united in their pursuit and can continually call each other to new heights. This is the subject of the next chapter.

I close with a quotation from Saint Aelred of Rievaulx, whose thought we will study more closely later. Here he makes a distinction between those with whom we seek friendship and those we love with supernatural charity:

> Divine authority commands that many more be received to the clasp of charity than to the embrace of friendship. By the law of charity we are ordered to welcome into the bosom of love not only our friends but also our enemies. But we call friends only those to whom we have no qualm about entrusting our heart and all its contents.[1]

---

[1] *Spiritual Friendship*, trans. Lawrence C. Braceland, S.J. (Collegeville, Minn.: Liturgical Press, 2010), bk. I, s. 32.

Questions for Discussion

1. Is self-image an important part of who a person is? Why?

2. Where does self-image come from?

3. What is the role (or should be the role) of friends in the development of self-image?

Questions for Personal Reflection

1. Is my self-image true to myself? How am I too critical of myself? How am I not critical enough of myself?

2. How do I receive affirmation from family and friends? Do I take it for granted, or do I receive it with gratitude?

3. How do I express affirmation for my loved ones? Do I assist them in true character assessment? How, or how not?

4

Friendship and Virtue:
Moral and Intellectual

Whoever fears the Lord directs his friendship aright, for as he is, so is his neighbor.

— Sirach 6:17

The thesis of this chapter is that it is with "friends" that persons form habits and develop their character, for better or for worse. I mark the word "friends" here because I am using the word very broadly. Here I mean anyone with whom we share our lives in some way. Almost everyone has friends in this sense. These are the people a person turns to in times of rejoicing and in times of trial, though how these people will respond will vary. It is with these people that a person develops habits—either good ones, called virtues, or bad ones, called vices. What kinds of habits are formed depends, of course, on several things, but especially on the moral practices of the persons involved. For it is a fundamental truth of human nature that people want to live and act *together with* their friends and that they will tend to act as their friends act.

It should be clear that the choice of friends is just about the most important decision a person makes. A person who has what we have been calling true friends will tend to grow in good habits, or virtues. A person who does not have good friends but instead associates with people not pursuing virtue will tend to form bad habits. The importance of this truth must not be underestimated.

What Do Friends Do?

Before proceeding to a more specific consideration of how true friends grow in virtue, let us turn again to Aristotle for an insight that will help us understand a little more about true friendship. In his treatment of friendship, Aristotle asks a very simple question: What do friends do together? In other words, given that friendship must surely be expressed in actions, what kind of actions most constitute the living out of friendship? Aristotle answers with two kinds of action: friends "do good for one another", and they "live together".[1]

The first of these comes as no surprise. Since a true friend wants what is best for the other, it makes sense that the true friend will work toward helping the other in whatever way possible. This is to *do good* for one another. The second kind of action mentioned by Aristotle might sound a little strange. Do friends always live together? If we understand "live together" properly, the answer is yes. This is the point we made above when we said that persons naturally want to live and act together with their friends. This is less a matter of *where* one lives than a matter of *how* one lives. Friends want to do the same kinds of things, and they want to do them together; they want particularly to share the most important things in their lives. Aristotle is insistent on this point. In fact, he emphasizes this even more than that friends do good for one another. He says: "For there is nothing so characteristic of friends as living together, since . . . even

[1] *Nicomachean Ethics* 1157b7.

those who are supremely happy desire to spend their days together."[2] We can say that friends want to live the same life together. To live the "same life" does not simply mean to live the same kind of life; it means to live literally the same life, enacting it together. As an analogy, this is not just about both being surgeons; it is about performing the same surgery. I want my friend to live a good life, the same kind of life that I want for myself. But more than this, I want to be good *together with* my friend; I want us to spend our days together; I want our lives to coincide in a very real way.

An excellent example—indeed, perhaps the best example there is—of an action in which friends want to share, and in which their lives can be said to coincide, is the action of conversation. We will consider the nature and importance of conversation later in this chapter. Here we might simply notice how conversation, when done well, can be an action that is so clearly not just "mine" but "ours".

We have seen, then, that there are two main ways of characterizing what friends do together: they do good for one another, and they live together, in the sense of sharing their lives together. If we look closely, we will see that at the root of both of these is a truth we keep coming back to: true friends must be mutually committed to pursuing the virtuous life. If two persons are really to be united in doing good for each other, they must share a vision of what life is all about. If they have different notions of what constitutes a life well lived, they will have different notions of what it means to do good for each other. True friends understand that the most important thing that they can do for each other is to help each other walk down the path of virtue. And, of course, as regards sharing their lives together, it can be a

[2] Ibid., 1157b19-21.

real sharing of lives only if they share a common vision of what they want to make of themselves in life.

We turn our attention now to how friends grow in virtue together, first as regards moral virtue and then as regards intellectual virtue.

Moral Virtues and Friendship

The seeds of virtue can be planted early in life, in the heart of a strong family life. Parents exercise the most formative influence in the early stages of character development. Yet, as noted in the previous chapter, as children grow, they begin to turn more and more to people outside the family. This is not to suggest that one cannot develop true friendships within one's family too! When a child develops such a friendship with a sibling, we can say that the relationship has gone beyond simply being siblings—as when, for instance, a person says, "My brother is also my best friend." A main concern for parents is whether their children are developing relationships with others who are committed to virtue. As I asserted at the beginning of this chapter, persons tend to become and act like those who are their friends in the broad sense. Let us take a little time to examine this point.

The term "peer pressure" usually signifies a negative influence that friends and associates can have on a person, usually a young person. Often parents rightly bolster their teenagers against the influence of bad peers by encouraging them to stand strong in their own convictions. "Be your own person and do not worry about the others" can be very fitting advice. Yet it is important to notice that the pressure or influence exerted by peers need not be negative. And the fact of being influenced by peers is not in itself something negative. It is very natural that persons be influenced by those around them, whether the person is young or old. In the case of the young, however, there is more at stake, because a young person is still maturing—which means that he is still becoming himself in very basic ways. As persons grow toward maturity, they turn to others for help and companionship. Thus, it is of particular importance that the young have friends of good moral character.

Let us consider two scenarios to illustrate how true friendship helps to develop moral virtue. Two young men, Francis and Thomas, are both convinced that goods of the soul are the most important human goods and that always doing the "right thing" is more important than riches, comfort, or the respect of others. They are just like any other person in their desire for companionship, and each wants to live his life together with others. Put more simply, each wants to have friends, at least in the broad sense. Now, Francis knows someone who fits our description of a true friend; this person shares Francis' desire for virtue, and he knows and cares for Francis as a person. Thomas, on the other hand, does not have such a companion but, rather, spends his days with others who do not share his desire for virtue. How each came to this point is irrelevant, as here I want simply to illustrate how helpful a true friendship is.

Francis has a significant advantage in the pursuit of virtue. First, in pursuing those things that are most important to him, he has peer companionship. The road to human greatness, to virtue, is a difficult, uphill grade. When the way to follow is not clear, his friend is there to help him discern the right path. When the way is clear but will require much sacrifice, his friend is there to encourage him and even shoulder the load with him. When it is tempting simply to turn back, to give up, his friend is there to say: "You can do it; we can do it."

We can be more specific. When Francis' complaining

about his neighbor starts to be uncharitable, his friend suggests assuming a different attitude. When conversation among the guys turns to inappropriate discussion of women, Francis and his friend support each other in an effort to change the topic. When Francis is suffering from the tragic death of a family member, his friend not only grieves with him but also helps him put the matter in the perspective of divine providence. This list can go on and on.

We need not go into great detail in considering Thomas' life. There are two main things to notice. First, if Thomas is in any of the above situations, it is very unlikely that he will receive the kind of assistance that Francis receives. In fact, he may well have to face negative pressure. When, like Francis, in a moment of weakness Thomas acts uncharitably, he may be joined and encouraged by his comrades. The difference is dramatic.

Growth in moral virtue is a project of monumental proportions. "Disciplining and reforming desires" sounds so simple. But how many really succeed? The words of Our Lord come to mind here: "Narrow the way and few there are who find it" (see Mt 7:14). What we are suggesting here is that friendship is one of the most critical natural helps to walking the straight and narrow path.

Friendship, the Intellectual Virtues, and Good Conversation

Wisdom was mentioned above as the most important example of an intellectual virtue. We should make a distinction between two different virtues, each of which can be called "wisdom".

There is what Aristotle calls "speculative wisdom". This

wisdom is a habit of insight into the highest truths of reality: truths about God, the universe, human nature, the meaning of life. This kind of wisdom, which from now on we will simply call "wisdom", is all about the kind of truths that one *contemplates*. Contemplation is a very special action in which a person fixes his mind's eye on something wonderful. Examples of contemplation are the monk who is absorbed in considering the infinite mercy of God, and the farmer who stops his work to consider how the beauty of nature reflects the glory of God.

The other kind of wisdom Aristotle calls "practical wisdom", and it is listed among the cardinal virtues as "prudence". The *Catechism of the Catholic Church* defines "prudence" as "the virtue that disposes practical reason to discern our true good in every circumstance and to choose the right means of achieving it" (1806). In other words, prudence is the habit of discerning the right way to act. It is the habit of judging what virtue requires of us in all the circumstances of life.

All intellectual virtues are habits of knowing or having insight. Wisdom is the virtue of insight into the highest realities, and prudence is the virtue of insight into how one should act.

Intellectual virtues, like moral virtues, are not easy to form; they require time and effort. Most everything said above regarding how friends support one another in forming moral virtues could be repeated about the intellectual virtues. It is not necessary to repeat those points. Rather, I want to focus our attention on something that Aristotle considers to be of central importance in friendship: the role of good conversation. Good conversation is, in fact, crucial for the formation of both moral and intellectual virtue, but let us consider the latter. Conversation is, or should be, about the communication of truth, which is nothing but a sharing of *insight*. Friends help one another to grow in insight and to grow in the habits of pursuing greater insight.

It has been said that our culture has lost the art of good conversation. There is, of course, no single cause at which to point a finger. Contemporary cultural habits, such as how we spend our free time and entertain ourselves, do not foster conversation. The near omnipresence of handheld devices has a deadening effect on conversation that is hard to calculate. Simply in the destruction of silent times we have lost the natural seedbed in which good conversations sprout. Further, families and friends gather around the television or other screens, if they even gather there, as opposed to around a fire, again removing a natural context for conversation. Many other high-tech forms of entertainment, such as the myriad "games" now played on computers, tend to isolate people. The general fast pace of society and the often engrossed attention given to practical endeavors, such as excelling in the marketplace, also remove the opportunities for conversation that were more abundant in a slower-paced society.

The influence of these trends and many other external factors should not be underestimated. At the same time, there are also serious internal factors—in other words, factors that pertain directly to one's character. Good conversation demands, and this should come as no surprise, a certain amount of moral virtue. What we are calling "good conversation" is an activity in which two or more persons come together to pursue truth. This communal pursuit of truth requires, among other virtues, humility, patience, and perseverance. Consider how difficult it is to have a good conversation with someone who is concerned more with image—how others view him—than with attaining the truth. And how can there be a good conversation with a person who, when the matter becomes difficult, says, "Oh well, I guess it doesn't really matter anyway"?

But there is more. In addition to the virtues that enable people to engage in a communal pursuit of truth, there must be some familiarity with the important matters to be discussed! This is of great significance. We need to feed our minds by study and good reading, and we need habits of reflection on the important matters of our lives and our faith. There should be an "interior conversation" within that extends to our conversations with others. Consider the words of Moses regarding the greatest commandment:

> Hear, O Israel: The LORD our God is one LORD; and you shall love the LORD your God with all your heart, and with all your soul, and with all your might. And these words which I command you this day shall be upon your heart; and you shall teach them diligently to your children, and shall talk of them when you sit in your house, and when you walk by the way, and when you lie down, and when you rise. (Deut 6:4–7)

And the psalmist says, "Blessed is the man [whose] delight is in the law of the LORD, and on his law he meditates day and night" (Ps 1:1–2). Those who ponder the law of the Lord day and night, and carry it in their hearts, are the persons who will want to discuss that law with friends. Indeed, they and their friends will have much to discuss! But how many of us find ourselves not having much of real significance to discuss? Our conversations, even with our friends, often revert to the weather, the economy, sports, or the latest tragedy reported in shocking detail in the news.

What can be done about this decline in good conversation? This is almost as difficult as asking what can be done about a decline in virtue. But let us take this opportunity to clarify a major theme of this book. Friendship is intimately linked with the highest human goods—particularly, moral and intellectual virtue. Friendship and virtue must ultimately be restored *together*. In other words, the more we develop virtue, the more we can exercise true friendship. And the more we exercise true friendship, the more we will grow in virtue, especially since true friends want nothing more than to grow in virtue together.

As regards good conversation, then, friendship is a critical aid. True friends want good conversations and will help one another and draw one another into good conversations. Friends will benefit from the insights of one another, as they constantly share the fruits of their personal meditation and contemplation. And, in fact, some truths will be discovered in conversation that neither friend would have discovered on his own. There is something irreplaceable about two minds working together, in a context of mutual affection and trust, to uncover the deepest truths.

Having said that friendship enables good conversation, we can look at the inverse and note that good conversation is very important for the growth of friendship. To the extent that we, either as individuals or as a community, work to bring about good conversation, we will be simultaneously enhancing the possibility for true friendships. Avoiding the negative external factors mentioned above, such as constant noise and distraction, is a critical first step. Beyond this, we can more and more accustom ourselves to the hard work of study—taken in a broad sense as something that everyone, not just students, can do—and meditation and prayer, which feed our minds and inflame our hearts. What is prayer, if not a good conversation with Our Lord? We will return to this point in the final chapter. Now we turn to some reflections on friendship and its relation to the larger community.

Questions for Discussion

1. Is friendship something I simply have or something I need to enact? Explain.

2. Why is friendship such a good context, even a necessary context, for the formation of moral virtues? (Make sure you remember what a moral virtue is.)

3. Read 1 Samuel 23:1–18. What might it mean that Jonathan "strengthened his [David's] hand in God"?

4. What is good conversation?

5. What are the necessary conditions for good conversation to occur?

Questions for Personal Reflection

1. Do the people I call friends help me grow in virtue?

2. Do I help the people I call friends to grow in virtue? How might I do this better?

3. How often do I have good conversations? If seldom, why?

5

Friendship and Society

When it goes well with the righteous, the city rejoices. . . .
By the blessing of the upright a city is exalted.

— Proverbs 11:10–11

Having achieved some understanding of the nature of friendship and its role in the development of human character, we
broaden our scope in this chapter to consider the connection between friendship and society. It might seem that this
is an unimportant side point about friendship. Aristotle and
Saint Thomas Aquinas think otherwise. To understand the
true significance of friendship in human life, and, indeed, to
understand human life itself, we need to consider the social
nature of the human person. Aristotle and Saint Thomas
hold that, as it is natural for a person to belong to a family
and a household, it is also natural for a person to belong to
a civil society. Let us consider first what civil society is, and
then we will be in a position to consider two things: why
a good civil society needs friendship, and why friendship
needs a good civil society.

What Is Civil Society?

The term "civil" is added to "society" to distinguish this
society from other communities or groups that can also be
called societies, such as the Church, a family, a club, or

some other organization. Civil society, which from now on we will simply call "society", is the society that the Greeks called the *polis* or city, and which today might be called the nation or country. This society is very different from any other kind of society because of its "self-sufficiency". In other words, only a society as large and complex as civil society is able to provide for all natural human needs, and thus, this society is what is called a "complete society". A family or a village can provide for many human needs and will normally suffice to keep people alive. But only a complete society, or civil society, which is, of course, much larger than a village, can provide for the fuller range of human needs.

A couple of examples here should make this clearer. It is only in a civil society that there can be a well-developed system of law. The rules of a household, important as they are, do not approach a full system of law; indeed, they are most effective *within* a society with a good system of law. It is also only in the context of a civil society that artistic and cultural expressions can be highly developed. It is for these and many other reasons that Aristotle says that a household or a village by itself might be able to provide for "life", but a civil society is required for the sake of a "good life". "Good life" in this context means human life with the various higher aspects that are achieved only through the communal effort of society. The great philosophers have a critical insight here. Human flourishing is so great and noble that it requires persons working together in a serious and complex fashion. Human civilization, though we tend to take it for granted, is no minor achievement! And true human civilization is all about enabling the highest refinement and perfection of human nature.

Hearing all this, one might reasonably ask the following

question: If people are going to work together for the greater perfection of human nature, do they not need to share a common vision of human greatness? The answer must be an affirmative one. In other words, if a society is to succeed in cultivating human nature well, then there needs to be at least a fundamental agreement regarding what constitutes human greatness, especially virtue. Most of the prevalent theories of civil society today emphasize the need for society to safeguard the freedom of individuals, rather than safeguarding the truth about the good life. Though this freedom is of the utmost importance, Aristotle and Saint Thomas would be quick to point out that civil society should be concerned with *much more* than freedom. The best civil society is one whose laws and structures are designed not only to protect life and freedom but also to provide a context for the growth of its members in true human flourishing.

To examine more specifically what this means and how it might be carried out would take us beyond the scope of our book. But in order to appreciate the relationship between society and friendship, it is important that we keep in mind that Aristotle and Saint Thomas held that a central criterion for evaluating a civil society is how well it promotes the virtue of its citizens.

Society Needs Friendship

Aristotle writes: "States, it seems, are maintained by friendship; and legislators are more zealous about it than about justice."[1] He proceeds to give a reason for this assertion. Of the utmost importance in a state are *unanimity* and *concord*; and friendship, more than anything else, brings about

[1] *Nicomachean Ethics* 1155a23.

unanimity and concord. This, it seems to me, is a brilliant point. We have seen how, in friendship, persons are united in their love of one another and in their love of virtue. Friends share a vision of the good life and strive together to achieve it. Friendships thus provide "mini communities" within the larger community; they are a basic unit, as it were, of striving for human greatness. In this way the mini community of friendship is very similar to the most basic, natural unit of society, the family or household.

Strong families that foster good morals and truths of human nature and faith provide the necessary foundation for a good civil society. Where, then, does friendship fit in? First, friendship *within* the family is an important aspect of the family's strength. And further, friendship *between* families, obviously most of all between parents, is what particularly strengthens those families and enables them to be more substantial units or cells of striving for greatness. Several families united by the bonds of friendship constitute, in fact, the healthy proximate environment in which persons live out most of their lives. It is among family and friends that we spend most of our time, and so also among them that we form our habits, be they good or bad.

An example will help illustrate the centrality of this community of family and friends in our lives. Consider a young man who goes off to serve his country in military service. He sees himself, and rightly so, as serving his country— the civil society in which he lives. But probably foremost in his mind as he goes to serve are his family and friends. In a very real way, when he is fighting to defend his country, he is fighting to preserve *their* way of life. He realizes that the common good of the civil society is the great good for which he is willing to sacrifice his life. Yet, at the same time, it is only natural that he focuses his attention on that mini community of persons among whom he has been formed and has lived most of his life. The point here is that a person has a place *in* the civil society *through* having a place among family and friends. Consider how absurd it would be for a person to say that his only community, his only place of belonging, is the national community—for example, the United States of America.

We can conclude that the character of the mini communities of family and friends determines the character of the national community, the civil society. Aristotle says that legislators are most concerned about fostering true friendship among citizens. How much sense this makes! To the extent that there is true friendship among citizens, society will be formed by persons, or groups of persons, united with one another in the pursuit of virtue.

Friendship Needs Society

What do we mean when we say that friendship needs society? We said before that the possibility of a good civil society is directly dependent on the existence of true friendships among citizens—the stronger and more widespread the friendships, the better the civil society. Here we make the opposite point: that true friendships are, to some extent, dependent on the existence of a good society. This dependence is different from, and not as absolute as, the opposite dependence. An example will help illustrate this point.

Let us compare the relation between friendship and civil society to the relation between a soccer player and a soccer team. A soccer team will never be excellent if it does not include at least some excellent, though not necessarily superstar, players. Similarly, a civil society will never be a truly good one if it does not include at least some men among whom there are true friendships. This much is clear.

The other direction seems a little less clear. Can there be an excellent soccer player without an excellent team? Clearly there can be such a situation, but we must look a little deeper. Perhaps right now an excellent player is stuck on a bad team. But how did that player become excellent? Soccer players will attest to the fact that a person cannot really *become* a good player without having played with good players on a good team. The famous Pelé did not become the player he was simply by kicking around a ball in the street, or even by playing with just a few of his buddies. By its nature, soccer is a communal activity, and thus, training in it is best done among a good "community" of players.

This points to a fundamental truth about friendship and civil society. A good civil society provides the natural context within which good friendships can grow. Now, I do not assert that it is impossible to form true friendships in a bad civil society. I do, however, assert two things. First, a good civil society provides significant help in forming true friendships. And second, to the extent that a civil society is not what it should be, men are hampered in their efforts, or have more to overcome, in forming true friendships.

We need not go into these points at great length. It is important, however, perhaps especially today, to have some appreciation of the difficulties associated with living in a society that falls short of being what it should be.

One of the most serious ways in which the flaws of a civil society are manifested is in its laws. It is hard to estimate the negative effect of bad laws on a society. Consider an example in the area of protecting human life. The negative effects of laws that permit abortion, for instance, are multiple. The first casualties are, of course, the unborn persons whose lives are forfeited. But not only does the law allow those particular lives to be lost; it also allows persons to form the evil habit of taking innocent life, a habit that can lead to the destruction of even more life and to the destruction of the moral character of the persons in question. Another example of a bad law that has serious negative consequences on several levels is the law permitting "no-fault divorce". Further, beyond allowing or forbidding actions, law also speaks to the community. Since it speaks of the judgment of the community regarding right and wrong in action, it has a formative effect on the judgment of citizens regarding right and wrong. For centuries, philosophers have referred to the "teaching aspect" of law. A society with bad laws, then, tends to form in its citizens, particularly in its youth, a corrupted judgment about right and wrong.

Besides in its laws, the flaws or strengths of a society are manifested in customs and cultural expressions. By "customs" I mean social habits that are passed down in a society from generation to generation. How the elderly are treated in a society, for instance, is not so much a matter of law as a matter of custom. How young men and young women interact, and the basic structures of dating or courtship, are also matters of custom in a society. But custom has a very similar effect to that of law. It has a formative influence on the personal habits and judgments of citizens. In a society in which there are, for instance, bad customs of how young men and women date, it is very difficult for youth, even those from good families, to swim against the current in this area. We will examine this more in chapter 7.

It is hard to comprehend the full extent of the influence that laws and customs of society have on the lives of citizens. Living in an age in which many societies reject basic principles of natural law and treat religious faith as something that must be kept completely out of the public square, many of us have simply become accustomed to "having to be different" from the society around us. But this is easier said than done. The fact is that a decadent civil society places unique obstacles to the project of seeking virtue and thus, also, the project of forming true friendships. These obstacles can be overcome, particularly through the help of supernatural grace. But obstacles they remain, and we must reckon with them constantly. It is small groups of families, united by bonds of friendship, that are in the best position to reckon with these obstacles.

True Friendship and Happiness

We could call friendship an art, acknowledging that it is something beautiful and noble *and* that it must be cultivated. It does not simply happen by itself. We noted earlier that a composer cultivates and develops his art through persistent, ordered effort. We could further call friendship the art *of happiness*, recognizing that it is not just one art among others. It has a unique position in its connection to virtue and holiness, to human fulfillment and happiness. To see this point is to see something essential about human persons (indeed, about any *persons*): their happiness is constituted by a union, or communion, of persons. It is for this reason that we can say that, in true friendship, virtue really becomes happiness.

What we have considered in this chapter has brought out another critical point: certain arts, particularly the nobler ones, can be achieved only through communal effort. It goes without saying that friendship requires a kind of communal effort. But we have seen here that friendship involves more than just the friends themselves. Let us think again of

Mozart. His excellence in the art of music came about because of his persistent effort in the context of his musical friends. But they were not working in a vacuum. Rather, they were the inheritors of a rich, noble tradition of music, passed down in a broad community that provided the necessary foundations for their work. Similarly, the art of friendship is something that needs to be passed down in certain ways (as, for instance, we are turning here to Aristotle and Saint Thomas for an understanding of it) and practiced by a larger community.

Our image of the soccer team can help us glean one final insight. We have noted the difficulty of becoming a good soccer player if one is not on a good team. But there is more to see here. What is soccer ultimately about, anyway? Is it about excellent players or excellent teams? Is it not the case that the very fulfillment of being an excellent player is to be an excellent player playing on an excellent team? Yes. What does this mean for friendship and society? Aristotle and Saint Thomas say that friendship finds its natural place and its fulfillment in a flourishing broader community. In other words, friends can most of all be what they want to be, and what they are called to be, exactly when they are members of a broader flourishing community. The Greeks had a wonderful insight. The height of human greatness is the greatness of a community, a community whose backbone is friendship.

It is important to note here that, as a Christian, Saint Thomas sees something that Aristotle could not see—namely, that there is a *supernatural* community, the Church, that is even higher than the civil society. What we have said about the civil society, the highest natural community, can and should be applied to the supernatural society. The Church needs good friendships, and friendships need the Church and find their fulfillment in her. Especially in an age of decadent civil society, it is a great joy and consolation for Christians to recall that they are, first of all, members of a supernatural community, a community against which the gates of hell shall not prevail.

Questions for Discussion

1. Why is it inhuman to "live alone"?

2. Why are friendships so important for the broader community or civil society?

3. Why is society important for friendships?

4. What extra challenges are there for people developing friendship in a decadent society? How might these challenges be met?

Questions for Personal Reflection

1. Do I recognize the extent of my dependence on others: friends, family, and society?

2. How do I act so as to build up the communities to which I belong?

3. Am I aware of the dangers of living in a society that does not value what I value? How do I respond to these dangers?

6

Discerning and Testing Friendship: The Wisdom of Saint Aelred

A friend is the partner of your soul, to whose spirit you join and link your own and so unite yourself as to wish to become one from two, to whom you commit yourself as to another self, from whom you conceal nothing, from whom you fear nothing.[1]

— Saint Aelred

Saint Aelred of Rievaulx, a Cistercian abbot in twelfth-century England, might seem an unlikely expert on friendship. But his *Spiritual Friendship* is perhaps the single greatest work on friendship in two millennia of Christianity. In this chapter, we will briefly examine two powerful aspects of his view of friendship between human persons. First, Saint Aelred holds that human friendship *has its origin and goal in divine friendship* and that this is the ultimate perspective for understanding human friendship. Second, he offers a very practical approach to discerning whether a relationship has what it takes to be a true friendship. Throughout this chapter, I will quote extensively from his book, as he has a remarkable clarity and force of expression.

---

[1] Aelred of Rievaulx, *Spiritual Friendship*, bk. III, s. 6.

A Divine Plan of Love

"All this begins with Christ, is advanced through Christ, and is perfected in Christ. The ascent does not seem too steep or too unnatural, then, from Christ's inspiring the love with which we love a friend to Christ's offering himself to us as the friend we may love."[2]

"All this." The reference is to everything about true friendship between human persons, which is the focus of Saint Aelred's book. *All of it* has its beginning in Christ, advances in Christ, and comes to completion in Christ. The root conviction in Saint Aelred's work is that human friendship is a gift from God that prepares us for the ultimate gift, friendship with God himself. This is an amazing assertion. Every single aspect of friendship, from its inception to its fulfillment—be it ever so challenging and rocky a road—is part of a highly intentional plan.

The notion is thrilling, and it can give us an entirely new perspective on the arduous good of friendship. There is more going on and more at stake than meets the eye. Have I been moved by someone, in some real way falling in love with that person? According to Saint Aelred, this has been inspired in me—usually without my knowing—by Christ. It goes both ways too. "He [Christ] inspires in friends that most holy affection."[3] Indeed Saint Aelred goes so far as to say that it is Christ who "kisses" us through the "kiss" of a friend!

We are immediately in deep, wonderful waters here, and we must try to understand this point rightly. If, as Saint

[2] Ibid., bk. II, s. 20.
[3] Ibid., bk. II, s. 26.

Aelred says, Christ is "the beginning and end of friendship", then we need to understand more just what this true friendship is. There is a strong compatibility between Saint Aelred's understanding of true friendship and that of Aristotle and Saint Thomas. Saint Aelred is well aware, for instance, that there are many relationships that go by the name "friendship" but do not deserve it. "Those who share a vested interest in vice falsely claim the fair name of friendship, because one who fails to love is not a friend. . . . Many are deceived by a counterfeit of friendship."[4] "Nor has anyone learned the meaning of friendship who wants any reward other than friendship itself."[5]

In Saint Aelred's mind, human friendship has the nature it does, and makes the demands it does, precisely because it ultimately is a stepping-stone to friendship with Christ. For Saint Aelred, the real foundation of such friendship is a shared love of God. The whole edifice, then, should be a further expression of the love for God, all aspects of the relationship being measured in view of its origin and end. "One must not hesitate to correct all the details on its [love for God] model."[6] Again, here we have a remarkable assertion: every aspect of true friendship is in some way an acting out of the root reality of each person's love for God.

Though Saint Aelred places human friendship squarely within this context of a divine plan of love, he gives much attention to the very things that Aristotle did. But rather than saying "though" here, I should say "because". The truth is that the Christian understanding of friendship gives it deeper roots and greater fruits. Saint Aelred has all the

[4] Ibid., bk. II, s. 54.
[5] Ibid., bk. II, s. 61.
[6] Ibid., bk. III, s. 5.

more reason to be very attentive to the requirements of true friendship, given its central place in a wondrous divine pedagogy—God's plan for the formation and transformation of his children.

Virtue and Knowledge

The student of Aristotle on friendship feels quite at home in reading *Spiritual Friendship*. We recall that Aristotle offers two reasons virtuous friendship is so rare: virtue itself is rare, and it takes a long time for two people really to get to know each other. Saint Aelred is certainly tuned in to this wavelength. "Friendship can rise among the good and progress among the better, but be consummated only among the perfect."[7] "We call friends only those to whom we have no qualm about entrusting our heart and all its contents, while these friends are bound to us in turn by the same inviolable law of loyalty and trustworthiness."[8]

Saint Aelred also gives much attention to how, given the rich nature of true friendship, it requires a certain character.

> As long as anyone purposely delights in evil or prefers dishonest to honest deeds, or as long as pleasure pleases a person more than purity, rashness more than restraint, and flattery more than chastisement, how is it right for such a one even to aspire to friendship, when it rises and grows from an esteem for another's virtue? If one is ignorant of the source from which friendship rises, it is difficult—indeed it is impossible—to taste even the beginnings of friendship.[9]

[7] Ibid., bk. II, s. 38.
[8] Ibid., bk. I, s. 32.
[9] Ibid., bk. II, s. 38.

Bracing words indeed! Yet Saint Aelred walks a fine line, and he is careful not to make friendship seem out of reach. After noting that friendship can grow and last only among those who are "good", he proceeds to clarify what he means:

> I call those "good" who within the limits of our mortal life *live sober, upright, and godly lives in this world* [Tit 2:12], wishing neither to exact anything shameful of another, nor, if asked, to offer anything shameful. I have no doubt that among such people friendships can arise, develop, and grow to perfection.[10]

To the person who, on learning the difficulty of friendship, finds his spirit flagging with discouragement, wondering if friendship could be worth all the trouble, Saint Aelred has strong words of encouragement: "What kind of wisdom is it to loathe friendship in order to avoid anxiety and to be carefree and absolved of fear? As if any virtue could be acquired or kept without anxiety!"[11]

So true friendship demands much regarding character in both parties and has, as Aristotle thought, a kind of minimum bar: that each person has a fundamental commitment to growing in virtue. Yet, as experience makes quite evident, having two "good" people who want friendship is not enough to ensure that there can or will be friendship. Friendship also requires a unique knowledge between persons. The fact is that all of us have a deep desire to know and be known. It is not that we need to know and be known by everyone. Rather, deep knowledge is part and parcel of the deeper communion we crave with those few special people. Perhaps at some point we have thought: "If only someone really understood what is going on in my life right now,

[10] Ibid., bk. II, s. 43.
[11] Ibid., bk. II, s. 49.

then I wouldn't feel so alone." This speaks to how mutual knowledge is a way of actually being together in the travails and joys of life.

We also should remember that sometimes, as two people come to know each other better, they discover that there is not the requisite compatibility between them for a deeper friendship. Saint Aelred notes, "It is especially useful for you to choose someone who suits your habits and harmonizes with your character."[12] Really knowing each other takes much time and requires seeing the other in various circumstances of life. The more we have seen how a person responds to various life situations, the more confidence we have that we really know who that person is. This brings us to Saint Aelred's specific considerations of the process of discernment.

Discerning True Friendship

"Surely you must first choose, then test, and finally admit someone considered right for such a trust. For friendship should be steadfast, and by being unwearied in affection, it should present an image of eternity."[13]

"Let his choice not follow the wantonness of affection but the insight of reason and be led by a resemblance of character and a regard for virtue."[14]

"You should not grow weary of caution."[15]

Perhaps Saint Aelred's fundamental conviction is that we need to be intentional about discerning friendship. This is not about being picky or choosy, as though we are simply

[12] Ibid., bk. III, s. 30.
[13] Ibid., bk. III, s. 6.
[14] Ibid., bk. III, s. 130.
[15] Ibid., bk. III, s. 74.

trying to avoid unpleasantness. True friendship is an arduous good, and it is won by those who are willing, in the
first place, to make the discernment that is commensurate
with the nature and nobility of the treasure being sought.

Before considering a few key specifics of the process that
Saint Aelred recommends, we can begin with a couple of
common pitfalls to avoid. The first one is striking: "Too
eager for friendship, he risks being deceived by its likeness,
accepting false for true, feigned for real, and carnal for spiritual."[16] We can be too eager for friendship. This might be a
bitter pill, given all that we have said about how friendship
is so worthy of being sought; it is understandable that we
would be eager for it! We might reflect here on the danger
that, in seeking friendship, we can become too preoccupied
with what *we* need and what *we* want. We must remember
that, in the end, friendship is never something we can demand, or earn, or simply go out and make happen. It is a
gift that we receive and a gift that we give. It comes when
we see, and are seen, and we are moved to give of ourselves
in love to another, for that other's sake; and vice versa. If we
are thinking first of ourselves and our needs, we are likely
to be too eager.

Saint Aelred proceeds to describe a mistake to which those
too eager for friendship are especially prone: we follow our
emotions without the proper guidance of reason. "Although
attachment frequently precedes friendship, it should never be
followed unless reason guides, honesty moderates, and justice rules."[17] Here, once again, we find a challenging truth.
We are often liable to form "attachments" that outpace and
even cloud our better judgment. "One must certainly guard

[16] Ibid., bk. II, s. 16.
[17] Ibid., bk. II, s. 57.

against a passionate outburst of love, which outstrips judgment and robs it of the power of discrimination."[18] This is something that experience shows to be all too common —and perhaps especially but not only in romantic relationships. Pursuing friendship is a delicate balance of being open to the promptings of the heart, while keeping oneself firmly grounded in a prudent assessment of the situation.

What Saint Aelred calls "childish friendships" can be the result of such "attachments without reason", and we should maintain a vigilant watch for such attachments, both in ourselves and in others toward us. Sometimes our vanity might hinder our seeing certain attentions we receive for what they are—the flattery or childish attentions characteristic of those who are immature or self-seeking.

Of the four steps in friendship that Saint Aelred enumerates, the first two are the most practical for our consideration; he calls them "choice" and "testing". In brief, first we make an initial choice regarding with whom to begin to pursue a friendship, and then and only then do we commence in earnest to test that friendship to see if we can go deeper.

Regarding choice, Saint Aelred emphasizes that there are certain characteristics that function as what we might call "disqualifiers" for true friendship. "Anyone entangled in certain vices will not long observe the laws and rights of friendship."[19] We should immediately remind ourselves that he is not advocating going through life with a high and mighty view of ourselves as somehow "beyond the reach" of many around us. Surely, in Saint Aelred's mind, we do well first to *examine ourselves* to determine how we stand as

[18] Ibid., bk. II, s. 75.
[19] Ibid., bk. III, s. 14.

regards these four characteristics that undermine friendship: irascibility, fickleness, suspiciousness, and verbosity. In his view, each of these four cuts at the root of some important aspect of what friends do together. I will give a quotation and brief comment on each of the four.

Irascibility: "It is difficult indeed for one often aroused by the passion of anger not sometimes to rebel against a friend. . . . Hence Scripture says, 'do not make friends with the hot-tempered or walk with the man of violence, lest you learn his ways and bring scandal to your soul' [Prov 22:24–25]."[20] Irascibility refers to having too much anger, or misdirected anger, or what might be unresolved anger from the past. Many of us have some "anger issues", but this clearly can be so to a degree that threatens the very possibility of true friendship.

Fickleness: "But how can there be any freedom from anxiety in the love of one who is tossed about in every wind and yields to every word of advice? Such a person can be compared to soft clay, in a single day receiving and manifesting varied and contrary impressions."[21] There is a great insight here regarding the need for a certain solidity of character in a friend. If he is to stand up as a reliable friend, a person really needs to know himself and be secure in who he is and what he wants, therein having genuine stability.

Suspiciousness: "A suspicious person is indeed constantly driven by curiosity. . . . For if he sees a friend conversing secretly with anyone at all, he suspects a betrayal. If the friend is kind or pleasant to another, he will exclaim that he is loved less. If a friend corrects him, he interprets that correction as hatred."[22] These are powerful words regarding something

[20] Ibid., bk. III, s. 15.
[21] Ibid., bk. III, s. 28.
[22] Ibid., bk. III, s. 29.

that many of us have experienced. The suspicious, jealous person simply "never relaxes",[23] and so a relationship can never be secure and at peace.

Verbosity: " 'Do you see someone who is in a hurry to speak?' asks the Wise One. 'The fool has more hope than he' [Prov 29:20]."[24] Saint Aelred gives no explanation of this one, other than noting that verbosity distracts from "due gravity". Surely some people are disposed to speak more and others speak less, yet there is a verbosity that indicates a lack of self-possession and judgment.

As regards the next step in discerning friendship, Saint Aelred writes, "In a friend, a certain four qualities should be tested: loyalty, right intention, discretion, and patience."[25] It seems he is thinking here that once we have confirmed a general possibility for friendship—by the absence of certain "red flags"—we now move on to a closer consideration of the possibility by testing for these key positive characteristics. Regarding each of these I will once again simply give a quotation and a brief thought.

Loyalty: "You may confidently entrust to the friend yourself and all that is yours."[26] Entrusting yourself and all that is yours is serious business, and it calls for the ability of each to be profoundly loyal. Enduring misfortune offers a good opportunity for proving and discovering loyalty. Saint Aelred also suggests that a friend's ability to keep secrets, big and little, is paramount and a key sign of loyalty.

Right intention: "From friendship the friend may expect nothing but good and the natural blessing of friendship."[27]

[23] Ibid.
[24] Ibid., bk. III, s. 30.
[25] Ibid., bk. III, s. 61.
[26] Ibid.
[27] Ibid.

Saint Aelred notes that we love ourselves without expecting some reward for it. Similarly, a true friend loves another as himself and is moved simply by that love and does not look for some reward.

Discretion: "A person may know . . . what should be offered and what should be asked of a friend, when to condole with or congratulate or even correct the friend, for what reason to do these things, and the right time and place for them."[28] The emphasis here is on a key aspect of friendship that we saw in Aristotle: that friends hold one another accountable. To hold another accountable requires insight, discernment, and prudence. Saint Aelred notes that when a friend corrects a friend, "his friend should not only see but feel that the correction comes not out of rancor but out of love."[29]

Patience: "When corrected, the friend may not fret or despise or hate the one who corrects him, and he himself may not be ashamed to bear any hardship for his friend."[30] The counterpart to the discretion to offer correction well is the patience to receive it well. How necessary both of these will be in any friend! Further, friends not only must be ready to suffer much with one another—they must be ready even to suffer much *from* one another. This can be the most intense of sufferings, requiring the greatest of patience.

I want to emphasize once more that being very cautious and thorough in choosing and testing is not simply to save ourselves from trouble later. Look at the opening quotation of this section. Saint Aelred roots the importance of choice and testing in how the fidelity of true friends is to be

[28] Ibid.
[29] Ibid., bk. III, s. 107.
[30] Ibid., bk. III, s. 61.

an image of eternity. We must be practical about discerning with whom we can really seek to achieve this great feat.

After choosing and testing, we move on to "accept" each other as friends. Saint Aelred is well aware that even careful testing does not rule out the possibility of finding in each other some of the very characteristics we were trying to avoid. Speaking of indiscretion, Saint Aelred writes, "If we have perhaps accepted such people into friendship, we must suffer them with patience."[31] He goes so far as to say, "Once a friend has been accepted, however, that friend is to be so tolerated, so treated, and so encouraged that as long as he does not depart irrevocably from the foundation you have built, he should be so much yours and you so much his in bodily as well as in spiritual matters that there should exist no separation of spirits, affection, will, or opinion."[32]

These are challenging words indeed, and they remind us of what friendship really is—an unselfish union and sharing. There is a real parallel to marriage here. Before fully entering into friendship, we must take great caution, and we need to be willing to let someone go, just as when discerning for marriage. Once we are "in friendship"—after choice and testing—then perseverance in fidelity comes to the fore. Marriage, of course, has an indissolubility all its own, but the analogy is still worth noting. Saint Aelred relates how he himself had to endure a friend's transgressions. Ultimately, choice and testing are means to an end, and they are part of trying to forge true friendship into a reality.

[31] Ibid., bk. III, s. 17.
[32] Ibid., bk. III, s. 7.

A Conclusion

Saint Aelred knows that the friendship of which he speaks is an arduous good that pushes human nature to its limits. Indeed, in a significant passage, he directly addresses the great paradox that a good so significant for human happiness seems almost beyond reach—as noted by the ancient philosophers. He writes:

> Since there is so much perfection in true friendship, no wonder those whom the ancients praised as true friends were so few. . . . Yet no Christian should despair of acquiring any virtue whatsoever, because in the Gospel the divine voice daily rings in our ears: "seek and you shall find" and so forth. No wonder the followers of true virtue were rare among the heathen, for they were ignorant of the Lord and giver of the virtues, of whom it was written, "the Lord of virtues, he is the king of glory" [Ps 24:10].[33]

These powerful words offer great encouragement. Ask and you shall receive; seek and you shall find; knock and it shall be opened unto you (see Mt 7:7). Here Saint Aelred places friendship at the heart of Christian life, suggesting that it must be an object of constant prayer. The Lord of virtues, and of friendship, seeks to share these choicest of blessings. We can ask, seek, and knock, so that he has the joy of sharing them.

For Saint Aelred, then, a Christian should see true friendship, in all of its many facets, as an integral part of striving after holiness. It is a beautiful part of the divine plan for sanctification, for preparing us for friendship with Christ. Saint Aelred goes so far as to say, "Friendship is the highest step toward perfection."[34] We will return to this point at the

[33] Ibid., bk. I, 25, s. 27.
[34] Ibid., bk. II, s. 15.

end of the book. We turn now to consider how the notion of true friendship helps in the understanding and practice of dating and marriage.

Questions for Discussion

1. For Saint Aelred, what is the larger context in which to understand the search for human friendship?

2. What does his emphasis on choice and testing highlight about the nature of true friendship?

3. In Saint Aelred's view, how does a Christian have a unique advantage in seeking true friendship?

Questions for Personal Reflection

1. Can I see the main relationships in my life as specifically chosen gifts from God?

2. Am I willing to take this challenging, intentional approach to friendship, being attentive to choice and testing? How might I do that better?

3. What can I do to make true friendship an important part of my prayer life?

7

Dating, Marriage, and Friendship

> But for the man there was not found a helper fit for him.
> So the LORD God caused a deep sleep to fall upon the
> man, and while he slept took one of his ribs and closed
> up its place with flesh; and the rib which the LORD God
> had taken from the man he made into a woman.
>
> — Genesis 2:20–22

The *Catechism of the Catholic Church*, in a section emphasizing the importance of proper preparation for marriage, states
the following:

> It is imperative to give suitable and timely instruction to
> young people, above all in the heart of their own families,
> about the dignity of married love, its role and exercise, so
> that, having learned the value of chastity, they will be able
> at a suitable age to engage in honorable courtship and en-
> ter upon a marriage of their own.[1]

In one rich sentence, the *Catechism* paints an excellent por-
trait of courtship, or what I will call dating, following a more
contemporary usage. First, it reveals the heart of the traditional understanding of dating—namely, the essential connection between dating and marriage. In other words, dating is fundamentally about preparation for holy matrimony.

---

[1] *CCC* 1632, quoting *Gaudium et Spes* (hereinafter *GS*), 49 § 3.

Further, the *Catechism* refers to two critical aspects of proper dating that stem from its essential relation to marriage: that it be honorable and that it be done at a suitable age.

We will consider these points to come to a better understanding of dating. The main thesis of this chapter is that true friendships help ensure that young men and women can engage in *honorable* dating, at the *proper time*, and that they will be prepared for the friendship of marriage.

Dating: What Is It?

We should first be conscious of different ways in which the word "dating" is used. Taking someone on a date can simply mean going out for coffee or to a movie. Thus, we can speak of dating and mean just this phenomenon of men and women going out together, either as a single couple or in larger groups. This sense of dating is not the main way that the word is used today. The more common meaning of "dating" is the situation in which a man and a woman, desiring to be with each other precisely as man and woman, develop a relationship that is more or less exclusive. This dating used to be called "going steady", which was usually the result of an explicit understanding. I will call it dating, regardless of whether there is an explicit agreement to be a couple or not. This relationship can be based on any of the three kinds of friendship we have discussed, of pleasure, utility, or true friendship; often it is a mixture. We will discuss this shortly.

Now, while many can agree to a general description of dating, there are diverse understandings of *what the purpose or goal of this relationship is*. I stated above that the key point in the quotation from the *Catechism* was that dating is fun-

damentally about *preparing for marriage*. This point has great
importance for us for two main reasons: (1) it tells us what
dating should really be, and (2) the vast majority of our society does not accept this point. Today, dating is often seen as
a way of expressing who I am or finding something I need,
or even as simply fun or recreational. And when it is seen as
a way to find a marriage partner, it is still often not seen as
a preparation for a covenant commitment. The contemporary incomprehension of the true purpose and meaning of
dating is particularly evident in *how* people date and in *when*
they date. On the other hand, as noted above, understanding
dating as a preparation for marriage means knowing how to
date ("honorably") and when to date ("at a suitable age").
We will consider each of these after looking first at the goal
of dating: marriage.

Marriage: A Unique Friendship
and More Than Friendship

One of the most striking aspects of marriage is that it should
be a unique instance of true friendship. The *Catechism* says
the following about marriage: "The matrimonial covenant,
by which a man and a woman establish between themselves
a partnership of the whole of life, is by its nature ordered
toward the good of the spouses and the procreation and edu-
cation of offspring."[2] A document of Vatican II has this to
say:

> Thus the man and woman, who "are no longer two but
> one" (Mt 19:6), help and serve each other by their mar-
> riage partnership; they become conscious of their unity

[2] Ibid., 1601, quoting Code of Canon Law, can. 1055 § 1.

and experience it more deeply from day to day. The intimate union of marriage, as a mutual giving of two persons, and the good of the children demand total fidelity from the spouses and require an unbreakable unity between them.[3]

We have characterized true friendship as a relationship between two persons who, wanting what is best for each other and working for each other's good, share their lives together. The above quotations emphasize these very points about marriage.

We do not have time here to consider the wonderfully complex subject of marriage at any length. There is one point, however, that we will insist upon here: spousal life lived to its fullness implies living a true friendship. Marriage is a union of persons who should help perfect each other and be fruitful. True friendship especially unites persons, perfects them, and allows them to be fruitful, according to their state in life. Now, spouses *can* be united through a mutual commitment of faithfulness without being friends in the fullest sense. Spouses *can* help perfect each other without being friends in the fullest sense. And they *can* be fruitful without being friends in the fullest sense. Indeed, even if they are not what we call virtuous friends, they are still bound by honor and moral obligation to live in a union of mutual helpfulness and fruitfulness.

But how much more united, mutually helpful, and fruitful are the spouses who have pursued the noble good of growing in virtuous friendship! How much *happier* are those spouses who strive with each other, more than with any other human person, to grow in love, to grow in virtue, to grow in wisdom. Realizing that they are called by God to work out their salvation *together*, they live a kind of shared life that is

[3] GS 48 § 3.

beyond the sharing possible for any other friendship in this life. The blessing of children is a kind of incarnation (literally, a putting into the flesh) of *their* love for each other. Their ability to raise and educate those children well is directly proportional to their success in growing together in virtue and wisdom. We might consider it this way: True love between spouses expresses itself first in their love for each other, which leads them to help each other to grow in virtue. This love, blessed by God, also bears fruit in the gift of children. This same love, which first bore fruit in mutual growth in virtue, continues to bear fruit in the proper raising and educating of children.

It is this understanding of marriage that should form our understanding of dating. If dating is a preparation for marriage, it should be conducted in such a way and at such a time as best to lead to marriage. Let us turn, then, to how to date.

How to Date

Just what it means to prepare for the vocation of marriage is more complex than it seems. The most basic aspect of dating is that we discern whom we will marry. It is, for obvious reasons, of the utmost importance that one carefully discern with whom to share one's very self and work out one's salvation. Yet dating is not simply about "finding the right person"—be that ever so important. It is also about *preparing oneself* to be married. Preparation in this sense includes honing those good habits, such as self-sacrifice and patience, that are critical to all true friendships. Further, it means growing in insight into the unique characteristics of a specifically nuptial relationship, such as exclusivity and total commitment. Dating, then, is much more than having an

enjoyable time, and it is more than seeking personal fulfillment. It is a very serious and beautiful enterprise, in which
two people develop as individuals and prepare themselves
for an irrevocable commitment.

As regards *how to date*, I have three suggestions. They can
be encapsulated as follows: (1) remember that you will only
have as much between you as you have above you; (2) show
charity through your chastity; and (3) date within a community.

Clearly, a main focus in a dating relationship is to get to
know the other person, and for the other person to get to
know you. But how is this done? It is not done by hours
of gazing into each other's eyes. Gazing into another's eyes
is meaningful when you already know that person. You get
to know each other best by standing next to each other and
looking outward, especially upward, together. You start to
share your *life* with the other person. You both start to enact life together by doing and discussing the most important
things in your lives. Meaningful conversations, which, as we
have seen, are essential in a true friendship, are also essential
in the dating relationship. Who are you? At the end of the
day, what gives meaning to your life? As a Christian who is
mature enough to be discerning a specific vocation in life,
the root answer is: your faith and your relationship with
Jesus Christ. But there is also more to you: What else do
you do, and enjoy, value, and desire? These things should
be done together and shared together with the other person.
In this way, you are in a good position to discern whether
the two of you are called to be spouses.

Our Lord said that where your treasure is, there will your
heart be also (Lk 12:34). If you slowly show each other what
you treasure, you will be showing each other your hearts.
There is nothing that unites two people like a shared com-

mitment to something great. A shared commitment to a promising career gives you a simple common goal; a shared commitment, however, to growing in character and holiness gives you a solid basis for the nuptial bond.

You show charity through your chastity. The point here is simple. One of the greatest challenges that dating couples face is the challenge to be chaste. A central aspect of what we mean here by "chaste" is a refraining from, as the *Catechism* calls them, "the expressions of affection that belong to married love" (2350). Here is a main way that those dating have the opportunity to demonstrate their unselfish love for each other. It goes without saying that the lack of willingness to control one's desires in this area is a sign that the relationship has a weak foundation, since it lacks a real commitment to the well-being of each other. Marriage should be a total self-donation in unselfish love. Unchastity, as a form of selfishness, attacks the dating and marriage relationship at its very root. Chastity, on the other hand, is an expression of true love. It is a gift that those who are dating give to each other, and it endures into and throughout marriage.

The best thing to do is to meet the challenge head-on. As a dating relationship progresses, couples should talk to each other about the importance of chastity. Physical intimacy should be seen as a natural sign of an *established commitment*. In this light, it is easy to see that premarital sex is always wrong. Even if I am "certain" that I am going to marry someone, if we have not yet made the marriage vow, then we do not have a real, permanent commitment. The focus of the time of dating, and engagement too, should be on developing a personal relationship in preparation for a permanent commitment, not on acting as though the commitment has already been made.

Consider this: Why are so many young men and women

seriously scarred when a dating relationship is broken off? One main reason is that premature physical expressions of affection have fostered a false sense of intimacy. One of the many benefits of chastity is the safeguarding of men and women from this scarring. In the event of a breakup, the couple who has been chaste is much more likely to separate in friendship, having experienced the joy of a relationship based in mutual goodwill and respect. Indeed, it is worth bearing in mind that very few people look back on a time of dating and think: "Gosh, I wish we had started kissing earlier." There are many who look back with regrets of another kind.

It is not within our scope to give universal guidelines for the expression of affection—although I do want to emphasize how important it is that individuals and couples look into this matter. See, for instance, the section of the *Catechism* entitled "The Vocation of Chastity" (2337ff.). In a culture in which the norm is to ignore these critical principles, honorable dating requires heroic effort and vigilance and the help of friends. On this note, we turn to our third suggestion: date within a community.

"Community" here should be taken to include the small community of one's truest friends, the community of family, and the broader local community beyond the family. What do I mean by dating "within" these communities? The focus here is not on where dating goes on, in the sense of a physical place—although that is a part of it. The issue here is more the spirit and attitude of dating. For instance, do two people see themselves as "on their own" in their dating? Is dating seen as something that is done in a vacuum and as something that is simply the couple's own business? Traditionally, dating was something that went on in the heart of the family. A young man would "come courting" and pursue a relationship with a young lady primarily within the confines of her home. Though that system might not have been perfect, it did have the benefit of the community aspect I am emphasizing.

The two keys to dating within a community are *support* and *accountability*. Dating obviously involves special challenges that friendship between men and friendship between women do not. The support of family and friends in the form of encouragement, advice, and so forth is a critical aid in meeting these challenges. Further, it is very beneficial for the couple to feel accountable to family and friends. This does not mean that family and friends interrogate the man and woman after each time they see each other. Rather, the point is that the couple should know that there are loved ones who want the best for them and expect the best from them. This accountability does not call for an overbearing, chaperoning presence. It does, however, call for the family and friends of the couple to seek to hold them to certain standards. This accountability means that a man and woman realize that they are not isolated individuals but are the object of a concerned love. And further, it is family and friends who are in the best position to provide an objective, outside view of a relationship. Advice from these persons who really know them is often indispensable to a couple. How many pitfalls can be avoided by dating within a community!

As already stated, dating within a community is primarily a matter of spirit and attitude, as opposed to where a couple spend their time. One example of how this can be lived out is in a woman's habit of discussing with certain family members or close friends the various aspects of dating in general, as well as specific challenges that she and her boyfriend are facing. Another example is in the effort that she makes to invite her boyfriend into her relationships with friends and family. This points to the fact that *where* a couple tends to spend time is, in fact, also very important.

I will be blunt here: I think that most dating couples spend too much time alone. Of course, time alone is very important in a dating relationship and is a good thing. But too much of a good thing can be a bad thing. Unfortunately, couples who spend too much time alone tend to have an attitude of separation or isolation from friends and community.

Here is a practical suggestion: Couples can resist the temptation to look upon time alone as the only "real time" that they spend together. They can cultivate habits of group interaction—interaction with friends, family, and larger communities, such as a parish. These groups are the natural context for discussing, praying, working, reading, recreating, and so forth. In this way, time alone might take on a more special character. It is seen as a special gift, a foretaste of the married state.

When to Date

As regards the right time for dating, the traditional wisdom is this: if you are not basically ready for marriage, then you are not ready to date. Again, by "dating" here I mean an ongoing romantic relationship. I do not include going on "dates", which can be an important context for healthy interaction of young men and women. A full treatment of what being "ready for marriage" means is beyond our scope. It can suffice to say that it includes both readiness in a material way and readiness in a spiritual way, or character and maturity. I suggest that, for many, though not all, this means not dating before the final year or so of college. It is not surprising that, in our society, young people are dating earlier and earlier.

If dating is simply about fun and personal fulfillment, then why not date early? Yet if dating is a serious preparation for the vocation of marriage, then there might be a very good reason to make the sacrifice of postponing dating.

But what is one to do in the meantime? Should one languish in isolation from the opposite sex before one is ready to be married? No. There is much to do and experience, that should be done and experienced *prior* to dating and marriage. Indeed, these things are essential preparations for dating and marriage. Here I offer two suggestions. First, it is essential that young men and women first develop healthy friendships with the same sex. In these friendships, young people can grow in maturity and develop the basic habits of personal relationships, without the challenge or distraction of the romantic element. Second, young men and women can develop habits of interaction with the opposite sex, yet primarily in the context of wholesome group activities, and in nonexclusive, nonromantic relationships.

Perhaps we should look a little more deeply into these two suggestions. One of the things that we have seen about friendship is that it does not just happen without much effort; it is like great art in this way. Friends-to-be must develop habits, for instance, of discerning the inner thoughts, desires, and needs of the other person, and often this is not easy. Now, we do not need a psychologist to tell us that this is particularly challenging in the case of a man and a woman —be it an explicitly romantic relationship or not (since, of course, a nonromantic relationship between a man and a woman could turn into a romantic one). Given the extra challenges in relationships with those of the opposite sex, it seems clear that a person can best develop the habits of friendship in the context that, particularly for young people, is naturally more welcoming and comfortable. It is not without reason that younger boys and girls tend to herd together among themselves. This is very natural. It is a sign of grave corruption that boys and girls today are being conditioned to become romantic and sexually aware earlier and earlier.

I am certainly not suggesting that boys and girls should not have contact with one another. In fact, they should develop nonromantic, nonexclusive relationships. Boys and girls both go through a stage when they prefer to be among their own sex. When they start to come out of this stage, normally as they enter the teen years, they have reached a very important moment in their lives. It is at this time that cultures traditionally were very attentive to guide the youth, to watch over and direct their desires and activities. Teenagers must begin to learn to interact with one another as honorable young men and women. For this end, young people benefit most from wholesome *group* activities. They need help in this area from mature, virtuous men and women, including their parents and older peers, who can act as role models and guides. This is where the family is so important. One of the great tragedies of contemporary culture is the way that teenagers and young adults leave their families behind in order to interact, alone and isolated, with their peers. The family itself, extended to include *its* relatives and friends, naturally provides the best context for young adults to interact with members of the opposite sex and thus grow in maturity.

But again, in the teenage years, and sometimes a few years beyond, the main focus should be on developing friendships *with the same sex*. Developing these relationships is itself a major factor in the process of maturation and thus in becoming ready for dating and marriage. We need to think more about these relationships and put more effort into them. As noted in chapter 2, central to human maturity is the ability to look beyond one's own needs and to consider what is simply good or best in itself. In other words, the heart of maturation involves growing in virtue. The experience of true friendship is critical for maturation and therefore is critical to being prepared for marriage, or even prepared for the *proximate preparation* for marriage—dating.

Please allow me to emphasize this: the conviction that young people should wait until they are truly ready before dating is rooted primarily in the dignity and beauty of dating as a preparation for marriage. This is not to be confused with a common contemporary attitude that says to postpone marriage so you can live your own life to the fullest first. This unfortunate attitude does not put off the fun of dating, but rather puts off the commitment of marriage. My position is also not to be confused with an overly scrupulous attitude of assuming the worst about oneself and thus persistently assuming that one is not ready for marriage. I do not suggest *indefinitely* postponing dating and marriage. I do suggest growing in maturity, virtue, and friendship *first*. So, when the time is right, by the grace of God, men and women will be able "to engage in honorable courtship and enter upon a marriage of their own". To do this in our society is to swim against the tide.

We turn now to consider the possibility of friendship with some very important people, of whom we might not have thought in terms of friendship.

Questions for Discussion

1. What does a true understanding of dating mean for *how* I (or those I love) should date?

2. How does a true understanding of dating affect *when* I (or those I love) should date?

3. How different is the contemporary practice of dating from a true understanding of dating?

Questions for Personal Reflection

1. Am I willing to be radically different from society in the area of dating? How might I do this?

2. What will help me act according to a true understanding of dating?

3. Can I explain and defend these points to those around me?

8

Friendship with Parents, Teachers, and Mentors

When equality exists the work of justice is done. For that reason equality is the goal of justice and the starting point of friendship. . . .

So by a kind of equality and likeness, which properly belong to friendship, people become and remain friends.

— Saint Thomas Aquinas
Commentary on Nicomachean Ethics

According to Aristotle and Saint Thomas Aquinas, any friendship consists in some kind of equality. There is a great insight here. To understand this, we should remember that friendship is always about living together, or sharing one life, to the extent that this is possible. This calls for an "equality" in the sense of a real likeness or sameness, so that two people can really be together. As a rule, likeness unites, and difference sets apart.

We can think of it this way: the more we are like another, the more we can really understand and enter into the other's life. Aristotle points out that where there is great difference—as, for instance, between the very wealthy and the very poor—it is difficult to be friends. It is important here to appreciate this with some nuance. The point is not that the wealthy and the poor cannot have any meaningful relationship with one another; of course they can. But we are speaking of friendship in a rich and proper sense. The more different our stations in life, and our habits, outlooks, and life experiences, the more difficult it will be to enter into each other's lives, understand each other, and live one life together.

This is a point that people with more life experience are usually able to comprehend better. Young people often have not yet had occasion to learn just how much is required in order to form and sustain a life-sharing bond. Many of us older people have had occasion, often with some dismay, to see how difficult it can be to see eye to eye with another, even in the context of genuine goodwill. For instance, sometimes the simple difference of having been raised in diverse cultures ends up being anything but simple. Perhaps we have seen that the idea "love can overcome any differences" is, in fact, a bit too simplistic.

Being "friends" in a loose sense with people from different walks of life is not the issue here. Let's remind ourselves that there are different ways of meaningfully relating to other people. First, we all should learn to relate with *friendliness* to everyone we encounter. We do this by being polite, respectful, charitable, and helpful in various ways. To be friendly is not the same as to be friends. It is a mistake to pretend to be friends with those who are not really our friends.

Second, we also have friendships of pleasure or utility— which can and should be lived honorably—with a wide variety of people in our lives. With some of these people, the relationship might grow into a deeper friendship, but with many it never will. This has to do with the limitations of human life and interaction, even apart from any issues of character. At the end of the day, we can really go deeper with only a few people. Finally, the nature of *true or virtuous friendship*, as going deeper and sharing more, shows itself as more challenging, demanding, and ultimately more rewarding. To understand these friendships, and to see that we can have them with some different kinds of people in our lives, we must grasp the proper importance of sameness, likeness, or "equality" in friendship.

The "Problem" of Difference

The fact that friendship requires and even consists in a certain sameness in life does not mean that there is no possibility of true friendship between those with real differences. Rather, for Aristotle the deep connection of friendship and sameness reveals a path to true friendship even in several key areas of life where there are necessarily notable differences between people. We will consider a few of them.

The relationship between parents and children is one of the central relationships in human life—from both sides. It is interesting that by the design of divine providence all of us experience, at least to some extent, the child-parent relationship. Not all of us experience the parent-child relationship, or at least not in its most obvious signification. For the moment, let us consider both sides under the name "parental relationship".

We should note first that it is not *by its nature* a friendship. In other words, this relationship does not include in its definition that parent and child are friends. This is obvious from the fact that a mother and her four-month-old baby are truly parent and child, but they are not in any meaningful way friends. Indeed, without intending to be wry, we can even ask: Are a mother and a fourteen-year-old really friends? The reality is that the parental relationship in itself does not constitute, nor does it immediately demand, that parent and child be friends. That parents and children often are not, and indeed sometimes cannot be, friends is a function of the nature of friendship and what it requires. So the great question arises: What does it take for parents and children to be true friends?

Aristotle and Saint Thomas have addressed this issue with characteristic nuance and insight, and their answer is beautiful. They address it in the context of reflecting on the point we considered above about how friendship always requires *sameness*. In their addressing the possibility of friendship between parents and children, they articulate principles that give insight into any friendships in which there are significant differences in the statuses or roles of the people in the relationship—such as between parent and child, teacher and student, mentor and mentored.

The key here is to remember the essence of any true friendship: it is about really living together in some rich way. Taking a closer look at parents and children, we discover that even as children mature into young adults, thereby becoming at least theoretically capable of true friendship, the reality is that there remains a wide gap in their life experience, self-understanding, and understanding of others—including one another! It is no surprise that many parents will affirm the depth of their love for their children while not claiming them as "friends". Simply on the intuitive level, the word often does not fit here because of a persistent gulf between persons, even though this is certainly among the closest of relationships.

I want to emphasize that there is something "natural" here —that is, in this difficulty in being friends—and we are not pointing to a problem. But that said, there is another side to the coin. Might we not find ourselves—and this from either side of the relationship—having a growing desire to share more, to come to an even deeper meeting of hearts? Dare we say that we want to move toward something of a more *equal* relationship? Here, I think, we touch upon one of the most poignant and beautiful of realities. There is a real possibility for parents and children to grow into a true friendship, *if certain things come to be*. But I will speak directly: in some cases, this simply will not come to be, for any of a number of reasons, some within human control, some not. Again, the reality of the parental relationship does not require such a friendship, and it can be the beautiful reality that it is even without such friendship ever being achieved.

Making Such a Friendship a Reality

The deep life sharing of friendship requires sameness, and some kind of "equality". Here Aristotle makes a pivotal distinction between strict equality and proportional equality. Without getting bogged down in the terminology, we can see a great truth. There can be a *real* equality and sameness even when not a *complete* equality and sameness. This principle is the key to understanding many things in life, especially the kinds of relationships we are examining.

In these relationships, the goal is not to obliterate the differences intrinsic to the relationship. That would, in fact, be the demise of the relationship. Perhaps in a well-intentioned effort to strengthen the relationship, some parents have sought to think and act like their children, only to find that their effort backfires. Parents are parents, and offspring are offspring, and this remains a governing truth in their relationship, permanently. What, then, do the wise mean by a "proportional equality" between parents and children?

Proportional equality, say Aristotle and Saint Thomas Aquinas, consists in the two sides *each truly loving in accord with the real differences between them.* There is more here than meets the eye. The principle behind this assertion is that *true love is rooted in true knowledge of the other.* Now, where there is significant difference, knowledge is more difficult, since knowing that which is different from oneself and one's experience requires much and is especially challenging.

Real friendship between parent and child becomes possible only when there is sufficient insight—on both sides—into just what it is to be the other person. While this is true in any real friendship, here this point must be emphasized because of the challenge presented by the significant difference between the two parties.

Thinking of real life will help clarify this. Consider a father and his son. The period during which the young man is growing into an adult can often be a time that stresses and stretches the relationship of father and son. There are surely many reasons for this, not least of which is that the young man transitions from being fully under the authority of his father to exercising an appropriate independence. One salient feature of this transition is the growth in knowledge in the son; he begins to experience and see the realities that his father has had to reckon with for years.

Take this one step further: perhaps now the son enters marriage and becomes a father. His worldview is seriously expanding. Imagine a moment one day—who knows exactly when it comes or if it comes at all—in which, perhaps all of sudden, scales drop from the son's eyes. Ah! This is what it is to be a man, a husband, and a father. This is what *my father* has been—for my mother, for me, for so long. Imagine the son turning to his father, and their eyes meeting. And they both know. Only now.

This might not happen in any given moment, but happen it can. And to the extent that this happens, a relationship of friendship is now much more of a reality between these two men. The son has come to a deeper knowledge of who and what his father is; he respects it and loves it, from the position of his sonship. The difference is not destroyed, but it has been bridged in a remarkable way.

The structure, then, is this: each side needs to know the difference, love according to the difference, and then live out that love. In the example above, I emphasized the drama of the son coming to know this difference, since naturally it will take more time for the child to come to such insight. Yet the father, too, needs to *know* and to love according to the difference. This cannot be taken for granted. Indeed, from the very beginning, a parent must learn to see offspring for who they are, according to where they are in life. Parents might have more work to do in this than they realize. Friendship is always a two-way street, even if it is sometimes easier for one side.

The relationship between teachers and students is another great example, and the same structure applies. A teacher and a student, as such, are not necessarily friends. They can have a real, functioning relationship without being friends. To become friends, both teacher and student will need to learn to understand the other and to see through the eyes of the other in significant ways. Usually, this requires more effort by the student than by the teacher. Yet again, it will demand much of the teacher, perhaps in ways he has not imagined.

To reiterate, here we have a different category of friendship. It is a *true* friendship; it can and should be rooted in virtue; it is about a real and deep sharing. But by its nature, there is a significant difference between the status or role of the persons, and indeed, a kind of hierarchy that must not be lost sight of. Such friends are not buddies and perhaps never will be. A teacher and a student who slap each other on the back like buddies have probably missed something of the reality of their relationship.

On the other hand, there is a real possibility that a person who *was* a student when younger can grow into being a peer of his former teacher. But note, here I say "former teacher". By comparison, there is no such thing as a former father. I myself have experienced the challenge of relating to a former teacher. We can be hesitant to leave behind the status, with its various trappings, such as modes of address, of being a student of the teacher. I do not think this should be frowned upon. The great reality of teacher and student, especially when it concerns significant aspects of life, is not something to underestimate. Perhaps *that relationship* does not endure; but perhaps it does.

To go back for a moment to the parental relationship, there is an amazing, almost breathtaking reality in how sometimes, in the circle of life, things can turn the other way. If my parent grows old and feeble, I, as his child, might experience being toward him something of what that parent had been toward me. What an astounding angle on life; things turn just enough to allow us to see something that perhaps otherwise we could not have seen and to do what otherwise we could not have done. But things are never really stood on their head. This man is still my daddy. And nothing will ever change that. I can be grateful that I got to see a little better, for what turned out to be a short time, through his eyes.

Friendship is always rooted in truth: in seeing it, loving according to it, and living it out. The more we see, the more we can love, and the more we can live.

The parent's or the teacher's role is to stand as a cause of great good to the offspring or the student. The role of the offspring or the student is more receptive and should include appropriate gratitude and respect. In any friendship, there must be mutual gratitude, yet here we see that the gratitude from the one side really should be greater than the other. That we do not normally associate these relationships with friendship is again a testimony to how friendship always stems from, and in a sense seeks, some kind of equality and sameness. But at the same time, Aristotle and Saint Thomas, recognizing this great truth, point the way to something that is a true friendship. Proportional equality is a real equality, and it puts such a relationship on a very solid footing.

And here we get a deeper sense of the amazing richness of human life, in the diverse friendships we can enjoy. If we are attentive to the nature of friendship, and the nuances of what these special relationships demand, we can perhaps experience a unique treasure.

Questions for Discussion

1. Why do all friendships require a kind of equality or sameness?

2. How can there be equality and sameness even amid inequality and difference?

3. What are the basic steps for friendship with parents or teachers?

Questions for Personal Reflection

1. Are there "unequal" relationships in my life—such as with parents or children, or teachers or students, or mentors or mentored—in which I might want to take steps toward making them friendships?

2. What steps might I take?

3. Are there relationships—perhaps with people very close to me—that probably will not become friendships but in which I can still do better than I am doing now?

9

Charity: Friendship
with God and Neighbor

I have called you friends.

—John 15:15

I suggested in the first chapter that Christians have two special motives for examining human friendship. The first is that an understanding of human friendship enhances our understanding of friendship with God. The second is that human friendship is a natural preparation for friendship with God. Now that we have spent some time examining human friendship, and have seen that Saint Aelred explicitly treats human friendship as a preparation for friendship with God, we are more ready to turn to the very perfection of the Christian life: supernatural charity, or friendship with God. After examining friendship with God, we will conclude by considering how this friendship transforms human friendship.

Charity as Friendship with God

We have emphasized that the main way of characterizing what friends do together (and really, friendship itself is all about what friends do together) is that they share their lives, or that they act together, particularly in such human actions as conversation. For Aristotle, this very point raised a serious problem when it came to a question of great significance: Can a human person have a friendship with a divine person? Aristotle gives an answer that is as crushing as it is insightful: no, human persons and God cannot be friends— because they are too different; their lives are too far apart. Now, from the viewpoint of natural reason—that is, reason unaided by divine revelation—this answer makes complete sense. Indeed, it is the correct answer for the human predicament *without grace*.

But something extraordinary happened, almost four hundred years after Aristotle's striking analysis of friendship. I like to think that the words of Aristotle were echoing in the ears of the God-Man when he was having his last heart-to-heart conversation, in this life, with his apostles. He said to them:

> These things I have spoken to you, that my joy may be in you, and that your joy may be full. This is my commandment, that you love one another as I have loved you. Greater love has no man than this, that a man lay down his life for his friends. [And now the line that would stop the heart of Aristotle:] You are my friends if you do what I command you. No longer do I call you servants, for the servant does not *know what his master is doing*; but I have called you friends, for all that I have heard from my Father *I have made known to you.* (Jn 15:11–15, emphasis added)

How dramatically have the actions of the God-Man, Jesus Christ, changed the human condition! Now, and only now, can man really be a friend of God in the full sense. Now man and God can be friends because God, first of all unilaterally, has shared his life with us. How wonderfully Jesus expresses this point when he says that now he calls us friends, "for all that I have heard from my Father I have made known to you"! We might say that he has invited us into the divine conversation itself. From the limited perspective of natural reason, from the noble Aristotle's perspective, this is beyond the dreams of man. We must never take friendship with God for granted, as though it could have been expected!

Let us turn to Saint Thomas Aquinas' understanding of the greatest of all virtues, charity. He asserts that charity itself is a friendship between man and God. He explains himself by reminding us of what we have learned from Aristotle: every friendship is based on a shared life. Now God has deigned to share his life (and here Saint Thomas literally says "his happiness") with us. Charity is nothing more than the mutual love between a human person and God that is based upon this shared life.[1] We saw in chapter 8 that Saint Thomas follows Aristotle in the conviction that every friendship requires some kind of equality. Remarkably, Saint Thomas raises this point as an objection against charity being a friendship with God; how can there be friendship where there is infinite distance, as between God and creature? Saint Thomas' reply to his own objection is stunning: "Charity is not of man in as much as he is man but in as much as, through the participation of grace, *he becomes God and a son of God.*"[2]

We can recall the lines from the Gospel of Saint John quoted above: "These things have I spoken to you, that my joy may be in you, and that your joy may be full." Our Lord shares himself by sharing with us everything he has heard from the Father, so that his joy, his happiness, might be ours. Now we can love him in a new kind of way. This is not simply the love of a lowly creature for an all-powerful

[1] See Thomas Aquinas, *Summa theologica* II-II, q. 23, art. 1 (hereafter cited as *ST*).

[2] *Quaestiones disputatae de virtutibus* q. 1, art. 2, reply 15 (emphasis added).

Creator, or of a servant for his master. This is the love of a friend for a friend. *This* love is called supernatural charity. *This* is possible only because God has shared his supernatural life with the soul. *This* is the highest of virtues. *This* is what endures, when all else has passed away.

From this vantage point, insights into our calling as Christians multiply. Let us consider a few of them. The Church has always taught that *mortal sin* deprives the soul of supernatural grace, which means, among other things, that the soul loses the supernatural virtue of charity. The *Catechism* states: "*Mortal sin* destroys charity in the heart of man by a grave violation of God's law; it turns man away from God, who is his ultimate end and his beatitude, by preferring an inferior good to him" (1855). We are now able to understand better *why* this love, the love of charity, is absolutely incompatible with mortal sin. We can put it this way: to commit a mortal sin is to act directly against the shared life of friendship.

We can see this point by looking to human friendship. We all know that there are certain ways of acting that would destroy any human friendship, such as stealing a friend's possessions. Similarly, mortal sins are actions that destroy friendship with God. The question might arise: Is this really the case in every kind of action that is considered seriously sinful? A look at Catholic moral theology from the outside might seem to reveal simply a long list of dos and don'ts. Is it really the case that there are so many ways in which a person can ruin his friendship with God? Let us look into this.

If friends have a common goal, and strive together toward it, then it is clear that they have fundamentally similar desires. In other words, as regards the most important things in life, and usually much more than just these, they have the same likes and dislikes. This point affords a critical insight into one of the central features of salvation history —*law*. Law is perhaps one of the most misunderstood of God's gifts to man. When Saint Thomas begins his famous treatise on law in the *Summa theologica*, he says that, at its root, law is a way in which God *instructs* man. Law instructs in the form of a command or a precept. But what does it instruct about? Law provides instruction regarding human goodness, or virtue, and how to achieve it.

Given this understanding of law, it should come as no surprise that the Old Testament Jews looked upon the law of God as a gift of incomparable worth. The great Psalm 119 (176 verses long) is a song of praise and thanksgiving to God for his law. It begins: "Blessed are those whose way is blameless, who walk in the law of the LORD!" The psalmist continues:

> You have commanded your precepts
>   to be kept diligently.
> O that my ways may be steadfast
>   in keeping your statutes!
> Then I shall not be put to shame,
>   having my eyes fixed on all your commandments.
> I will praise you with an upright heart,
>   when I learn your righteous ordinances.
> I will observe your statutes;
>   O forsake me not utterly! . . .
>
> With my whole heart I seek you;
>   let me not wander from your commandments!
> I have laid up your word in my heart,
>   that I might not sin against you.
> Blessed are you, O LORD;
>   teach me your statutes!
> With my lips I declare
>   all the ordinances of your mouth.

In the way of your testimonies I delight
　　as much as in all riches.
I will meditate on your precepts,
　　and fix my eyes on your ways.
I will delight in your statutes;
　　I will not forget your word. (vv. 4–16)

The law was seen as guiding the people to what was at one and the same time a truly good life and a life most pleasing to God.

Now if, in the New Testament, God calls man to friendship with himself, this sheds new light on the importance of God's law. We can see God's law as directing toward, and preparing for, friendship with himself. We can say that his law provides the necessary guidelines for friendship; it points to how we can "share our lives" with him. This is how we should look upon his law—whether it be the precepts given in the New Testament, the natural law written in our hearts, or the laws of the Church. (Saint Thomas explains that the law of the Old Testament was a preparation for the law of the New Testament.)[3]

The importance of this point should not be underestimated. Is this not a most beautiful and consoling insight? God asks so much of me, as regards how I act, because he wants me to live as his friend! Saint Thomas insists on this point. He says that "the chief intention of the divine law is to establish man in friendship with God."[4] He explains that "there cannot be any friendship of man to God, who is supremely good, unless man become good. . . . But the goodness of man is virtue."[5] In other words, friend-

---

[3] See *ST* I-II, q. 107, art. 1 and 2.
[4] *ST* I-II, q. 99, art. 2.
[5] Ibid.

ship with God, like any friendship, always demands certain things. And the role of law is to instruct us in what those things are. Saint Thomas ties this in with what we have seen above, when he argues that supernatural charity cannot exist without obedience to the law of God. Here is his striking argument:

> For it is written (1 John 2:4, 5): "He who saith that he knoweth God, and keepeth not his commandments, is a liar . . . but he that keepeth his word, in him in very deed the charity of God is perfected": and this because friends have the same likes and dislikes.[6]

Friends have the same likes and dislikes. This is the final word on why God has given us a law and on why charity is incompatible with mortal sin.

This is also the final word on why Aristotle was correct in asserting that *to be virtuous is to be happy.* Recall that to have a virtue is not only to act in certain ways. It is also to *want* to act in these ways and to *enjoy* it. God calls us to virtue, to the transformation of our desires and actions, *so that we might be completely united with him in our desires and actions.* And thus (and here again is something Aristotle could never have foreseen), God calls us *to make the supernatural virtue of charity the root of all virtues.*[7] Charity, supernatural love for him, should be *the inspiration, and the end or goal, of everything we desire and do.* Charity is the perfection of the Christian life, for the Christian life is about friendship with God.

Our consideration of friendship with God also gives us insight into our *prayer life,* or more broadly, our *interior life.* Just as conversation is at the heart of human friendship, so it is at the heart of a person's friendship with God. We spoke

[6] *ST* II-II, q. 104, art. 3.
[7] See ibid. q. 23, art. 7 and 8.

earlier of the unique beauty of the conversation of friends; there is no conversation like the conversation of persons united by their love for each other and their love for virtue. Friends' speech with one another is marked by an ease, a comfort, and a joy, and also an attentiveness and a seriousness not found in other speech. This conversation of human friends provides a model, though not a perfect one, for the conversation that we can and should have with God. Saint Thomas speaks of the interior life of the person in the state of grace as a conversation with God and the angels. He says that this conversation, while imperfect in this life, will be brought to complete fullness in the life of heaven.[8]

As we look at our own prayer lives, we might ask ourselves a few questions. First and most importantly, do I look upon conversation with God as essential to my relationship with him and thus as something that I should work on unceasingly? Good habits are formed only through the repeated exercise of good actions. Second, do I participate in liturgical prayer (the Mass, the sacraments, and the Liturgy of the Hours) with a spirit of entering into a unique mode of conversation with my divine friend? The *Catechism* states:

> The liturgy is also the participation in Christ's own prayer addressed to the Father in the Holy Spirit. In the liturgy, all Christian prayer finds its source and goal. Through the liturgy the inner man is rooted and grounded in "the great love with which [the Father] loved us" in his beloved Son (Eph 2:4; 3:16–17). It is the same "marvelous work of God" that is lived and internalized by all prayer, "at all times in the Spirit" (Eph 6:18). (1073)

Third, do I seek throughout my day to turn my heart and my mind to my divine friend, for the kind of personal contact to which he has invited us?

[8] Ibid., q. 23, art. 1.

It should be noted that those with an authentic friendship with God always retain a proper respect for his divine majesty. We do not give a "slap on the back" to our divine friend. He calls us to the most intimate of relationships, but it remains a relationship between the All Holy and a sinner, between Creator and creature, between Father and son. A son always retains a reverence for his father. Our reflections here should not be construed as suggesting that we treat God as "one of the boys". Friendship with God is literally an awesome reality. It is an unmerited gift. It should be approached with the appropriate sentiments of reverence, thanksgiving, and wondrous joy.

Charity as Friendship with God, Extended to Other Persons

Where does our neighbor fit into the Christian understanding of charity, especially since charity is friendship with God? Christians have always held that there are two objects of charity: God and neighbor. The key to understanding charity toward neighbor is to understand how these two objects of charity are related to each other. This is a somewhat subtle yet extremely important point. God and neighbor are both objects of charity, but in such a way that there is really only *one* love here. How is this possible? God is the primary object of charity, and man is the secondary object. When I say "primary" here, I mean two things. First, God is loved more than neighbor, and second, God is *the very reason for the love of neighbor.*

Charity is first a love of God, above all things and for his own sake. God is seen as most worthy and lovable, as the source of goodness, and as goodness itself. As noted above, charity is a love for God that is possible only in the context of God's sharing his life and his happiness with us. Now, when one loves God with this love of charity, one will also want *other persons to share in the life of God*. Since God has called all persons to share in his life, a person with charity loves all persons, wanting them to "live with God". The heart of charity for neighbor is the desire for the neighbor to share in God's life, to live with him in friendship.

We receive further insight into this point when we consider that charity extends even to our enemies. Saint Thomas turns again to his understanding of friendship in order to explain.

> When a man has friendship for a certain person, for his sake he loves all belonging to him, be they children, servants, or connected with him in any way. Indeed, so much do we love our friends, that for their sake we love all who belong to them, even if they hurt or hate us; so that, in this way the friendship of charity extends even to our enemies, whom we love out of charity in relation to God, to whom the friendship of charity is chiefly directed.[9]

What a beautiful insight into true friendship! Love for a friend extends even beyond that friend; it extends to the friend's friends, family, and so forth. Of course, this does not mean that the friends of the friend are immediately loved because of who they are in themselves. The friends of the friend are loved *as being* the friends of the friend (though that relationship might then also become something more). In the case of charity, a person loves his enemies as persons called to friendship with God. As one grows in charity, one grows in the ability to look upon other persons precisely as the beloved children of God.

Consider the example of a person who was filled with

[9] Ibid., q. 23, art. 1, reply 2.

charity: Mother Teresa of Calcutta. What did she see when she looked upon a fellow man? She saw Christ. And further, she saw a beloved of Christ, one called to live his life with him. This is supernatural charity in action, the love of God extended to our neighbor. The *Catechism* states: "Charity is the theological virtue by which we love God above all things for his own sake, and our neighbor as ourselves for the love of God" (1822).

Some Final Thoughts on Human Friendships and Friendship with God

Aristotle was convinced that human perfection, or human happiness, is normally attained only in the context of human friendships. We must remember that true friendship *with God* is something that Aristotle could not have imagined. The supernatural gift of friendship with God infinitely surpasses the greatest perfection that unaided human nature can achieve. We have noted how human friendships can prepare for supernatural friendship by helping us understand what friendship is and by helping us develop habits of friendship, of "living together" with friends. But a question arises: Is charity, friendship with God and neighbor, something that is simply added "on top of" human friendships? Is human friendship, then, replaced by supernatural charity, now that there is something much higher and more important? The answer is no.

Charity transforms and raises up natural human friendship. In other words, with charity, the human friendship that has been the main topic of this book *is given deeper roots and greater fruits*. This is the perspective we discovered in Saint Aelred. Christians seek to grow in human friendship in the context of charity, and ultimately in view of deepening their relationship with Christ. The supernatural life of Christians gives them that much more as a common basis for their friendship, as well as that much more to look forward to and to enjoy together as friends.

Let us consider this special situation of Christians as regards human friendship. Christianity provides a deeper understanding of such crucial realities as virtue and law. It also provides a much greater incentive to be virtuous— the personal invitation of the Creator, accompanied by the promise of his assistance through the Church and her sacraments. These things make a significant difference in the journey toward virtue and holiness, which is the very journey that friends seek to make together.

Friends always want to be together, and they naturally dread separation. Christianity provides supernatural hope, and the promise that the ultimate life that they share transcends the mortal life of this world. Indeed, this ultimate life is not a mortal life at all; it is the life of the Blessed Trinity. What greater joy is there for those with a human friendship than to know that, united in charity, they *share together* in the life of God himself.

Questions for Discussion

1. What is charity?

2. How is it possible for a human person to be a friend of God?

3. Why does God give us laws?

4. How does the importance of conversation in friendship apply to friendship with God?

5. Does charity necessarily extend to my neighbor? Why?

6. How does supernatural charity transform human friendships?

Questions for Personal Reflection

1. Do I live as though friendship with God is the goal of my life—*in this life*?

2. Is my prayer life recognizable as a conversation between friends? How might I work on this?

3. Does my love for God truly extend to my neighbors? To the extent that it does not, why does it not?

Exercise

Read the following Scripture passages and meditate upon the friendship that Our Lord had with human persons as he walked among us as a man: Mark 6:30–32; John 6 (the "bread of life" discourse), especially verses 66–71; John 11 (the raising of Lazarus), especially verses 28–44; John

13–17 (the Last Supper and Jesus' last discourse), especially 13:1; 23–25; 14:27–28; 15:11–15; 16:22; 17:6–19; Matthew 26:36–46 (Jesus in Gethsemane).

Friendship in This Life and in the Next

In the section of the *Summa theologica* called the "treatise on happiness" (the first five questions of the First Part of the Second Part), Saint Thomas asks a question pertinent to our study: Is the fellowship of friends necessary for happiness?[1] As is often the case when Saint Thomas answers such questions, he responds that we must a make a distinction. We distinguish between the happiness of this life and the happiness of the next life. As regards the happiness that can be achieved in this life, he says, along with Aristotle, that a happy man *must have* true friends. He explains that happy persons need friends so that they will be able to "act well". In other words, if one is really to act or live as a good, happy person does, one needs the fellowship of friends.

Saint Thomas lists three reasons why a person needs friends: (1) so that the person can "do good" to them, (2) so that the person may delight in seeing them do good, and (3) so that the person may be helped by them in living well. He explains the third point with this sweeping assertion: "For in order that man may do well, whether in the works of the active life, or in those of the contemplative life, he needs the fellowship of friends."

Let us think about this. To *do well*, whether in the works

[1] *ST* I-II, q. 4, art. 8.

of the "active life", which is especially associated with the moral virtues, or in the works of the "contemplative life", which is especially associated with the intellectual virtues, a person *must* have friends. Thus, in this life, we can be virtuous, and therefore happy, only if we have developed virtuous friendships with others.

But what about the next life, the life of the Beatific Vision in heaven? Saint Thomas makes clear that even if there were only one soul in heaven, that soul would be in a perfectly happy union with God. Thus, *human* friendship is not absolutely essential to the ultimate happiness of heaven. This is not the complete picture, however. There *will* be other souls there, and one will have friendships with them. Saint Thomas almost seems torn in expressing just how wonderful this will be, because he does not want to imply that there could be anything lacking in the central relationship with God himself. In other words, if Saint Thomas makes friendship with other humans in heaven sound too important, it might make it seem as if friendship with God does not completely satisfy our desires. Yet he indicates that friendship with other humans will be a part of that inexpressible fullness of happiness. He quotes Saint Augustine of Hippo, who says that those in heaven will "see one another and rejoice in God at their fellowship".

For help in savoring this point, let us turn once more to the great Saint Aelred of Rievaulx. He concludes *Spiritual Friendship* with a sort of litany of the blessings of friendship. This litany culminates—and how fitting this is—in a consideration of the *prayer of friends* for one another, and how prayer lifts them toward their ultimate union in Christ.

> Surpassing all this is prayer for each other. In remembering a friend, the more lovingly one sends forth prayer to God, with tears welling up from fear or affection or grief,

the more effective that prayer will be. Thus praying to Christ for a friend and desiring to be heard by Christ for a friend, we focus on Christ with love and longing. Then sometimes suddenly, imperceptibly, affection melts into affection, and somehow touching the sweetness of Christ nearby, one begins to taste how dear he is and experience how sweet he is.[2]

We see here once again the stunning beauty of God's plan! Moved either by some great suffering or simply by affection, we are in earnest prayer for a friend. Is it not true that love for others especially moves us to prayer? This can give us new insight into how God's loving plan includes those painful situations that move us to urgent prayer. Then in that prayer, drawing close to Christ as we focus on him "with love and longing", something amazing happens. In that closeness to Christ *we discover in a new way the sweetness of Christ himself*! Remember, Saint Aelred said that from the start, human friendship is a way in which Christ draws us to himself.

So, in reverent silence before so great a gift and mystery, I close this book with the words with which Saint Aelred closes his book:

Thus rising from that holy love with which a friend embraces a friend to that with which a friend embraces Christ, one may take the spiritual fruit of friendship fully and joyfully into the mouth, while looking forward to all abundance in the life to come. When the fear is dispelled that now fills us with dread and anxiety for one another, when the hardship is removed that we must now endure for one another, when, moreover, along with death the sting of death is removed—the sting that so often pierces and distresses us and makes us grieve for one another—then with

[2] *Spiritual Friendship*, bk. III, s. 133.

the beginning of relief from care we shall rejoice in the supreme and eternal good, when the friendship to which on earth we admit but few will pour out over all and flow back to God from all, for God will be all in all.[3]

---

[3] Ibid., bk. III, s. 134.

A Gospel Meditation

The next day again John was standing with two of his disciples; and he looked at Jesus as he walked, and said, "Behold, the Lamb of God!" The two disciples heard him say this, and they followed Jesus. Jesus turned, and saw them following, and said to them, "What do you seek?" And they said to him, "Rabbi" (which means Teacher), "where are you staying?" He said to them, "Come and see." They came and saw where he was staying; and they stayed with him that day, for it was about the tenth hour.

—John 1:35–39

The story is a familiar one. Jesus had walked by on the previous day, and John the Baptist had pointed him out as the Lamb of God. That day, none of John's disciples followed Jesus. This day, Jesus once again walks by, and John once again bears witness to the Lamb of God. It is clear enough what Jesus is hoping for. How many times will he have to walk by before someone follows him? This day, John and Andrew arise and follow the Lord. Jesus has not as yet had any personal contact or opened his mouth in discourse with any of the men who will be his disciples. Feel the excitement of the fisher of men: his first two fish are on the line. Hardly able to contain himself, he soon turns and asks *the question*; it is always the first question for those who would follow him: What do you seek? He must have an answer; all depends on it.

The answer given is all that he had hoped for, all that he had dreamed of. Given in a startled moment, it says it all. "Rabbi, Master"—they recognize him as a teacher, one to learn from, one to follow—"where do you live?" *He* is what they want. They want to be with him, they want to share their lives with him. Nothing more, nothing less.

Oh, how this fits with his desires! He solemnly extends an invitation. The Eternal Word of God, Yahweh himself, has become man that he might deliver *this* invitation: "Come and see." What more can he say? What more can God offer to man? "Come, and see, *where I live.* For where I am, there would I have you be. Be not surprised when you first see my dwelling. It does not look like the dwelling of your kings. Indeed, at times it will be a little uncomfortable for you. But place your trust in me. And I, the Lord of Hosts, swear by my very self that you will find it to be a home, your home."

Our Lord has extended a call to friendship. What do friends do? They *share their lives.* But how can a human person live as God lives? There is only one answer, the one that the Lord Jesus gives: he must come and see. And how few there are who do it, for the road is narrow and is not easy. During this life, there are many hindrances to living out this friendship, the friendship of supernatural charity. Indeed, the Lord warned that unless a person is willing to take up his cross, that person is not worthy of him. That is, they cannot *live together,* as friends do.

But to the one who comes and sees, lives and perseveres —to this one the Lord will give all. And one great day, having run the race, this person will stand before the judgment seat of the Almighty, having during this life striven to live a friendship with the One he has seen only through a glass and darkly.

Then the mighty Judge will ask, "What is it you seek?"

"Master, where do you live?"

"My friend, come, and *see*."

Sources Cited

Aelred of Rievaulx. *Spiritual Friendship*. Translated by Lawrence C. Braceland, S.J. Collegeville, Minn.: Liturgical Press, 2010.

Aquinas, Thomas. *Commentary on Aristotle's Nicomachean Ethics*. Translated by C. I. Litzinger. Notre Dame: Dumb Ox Books, 1993.

——. *On Charity* [from *Quaestiones disputatae de virtutibus*]. Translated by Lottie H. Kendzierski. Milwaukee, Wis.: Marquette University Press, 1997.

——. *Summa Theologica of St. Thomas Aquinas*. Translated by Fathers of the English Dominican Province. Westminster, Md.: Christian Classics, 1981.

Aristotle. *Nicomachean Ethics*. In *The Basic Works of Aristotle*. Edited by Richard McKeon. New York: Random House, 1941.

Augustine of Hippo. *Confessions*. Translated by F. J. Sheed. Indianapolis: Hackett Publishing, 1993.

Plato. *Plato: Five Dialogues*. Translated by G. M. A. Grube. Indianapolis: Hackett Publishing, 1981.

Second Vatican Council. *Gaudium et Spes*. In *Vatican Council II: The Conciliar Documents*, edited by Austin Flannery, O.P. Northport, N.Y.: Costello Publishing, 1998.

Further Reading

Author's Blog

LifeCraft. http://life-craft.org.

About Friendship

Aelred of Rievaulx. *Spiritual Friendship.* Translated by Lawrence C. Braceland, S.J. Collegeville, Minn.: Liturgical Press, 2010.

Aquinas, Thomas. *Commentary on Aristotle's Nicomachean Ethics.* Translated by C. I. Litzinger. Notre Dame: Dumb Ox Books, 1993. See the commentary on books 8 and 9.

———. *Summa Theologica of St. Thomas Aquinas* II–II. Translated by Fathers of the English Dominican Province. Westminster, Md.: Christian Classics, 1981. QQ. 23–33 (on supernatural charity).

Aristotle. *Nicomachean Ethics.* In *The Basic Works of Aristotle.* Edited by Richard McKeon. New York: Random House, 1941. Bks. 8–9.

Lewis, C. S. *The Four Loves*. New York: HarperCollins, 2017.

About Virtue

Aquinas, Thomas. *Summa Theologica of St. Thomas Aquinas* I-II. Translated by Fathers of the English Dominican Province. Westminster, Md.: Christian Classics, 1981. QQ. 49–67.

Cessario, Romanus, O.P. *The Moral Virtues and Theological Ethics*. Notre Dame, Ind.: University of Notre Dame Press, 2008.

Gray, Tim, and Curtis Martin. *Boys to Men: The Transforming Power of Virtue*. Steubenville, Ohio: Emmaus Road Publishing, 2001.

Kreeft, Peter. *Back to Virtue*. San Francisco: Ignatius Press, 1992.

McInerny, Ralph. *Ethica Thomistica: The Moral Philosophy of Thomas Aquinas*. Washington, D.C.: Catholic University of America Press, 1997.

Pieper, Josef. *The Four Cardinal Virtues*. Notre Dame, Ind.: University of Notre Dame Press, 1966.

———. *Faith, Hope, Love*. San Francisco: Ignatius Press, 1997.

About Saint Thomas Aquinas

Chesterton, G. K. *Saint Thomas Aquinas* and *Saint Francis of Assisi*. San Francisco: Ignatius Press, 2002.

Pieper, Josef. *Guide to Thomas Aquinas*. San Francisco: Ignatius Press, 1991.